LANDSCAPE
DESIGN
FOR THE
HOME OWNER

WITH

LYNTON JOHNSON

Published by **Briza Publications**

CK/1990/11690/23

P.O. Box 56569
Arcadia
0007
Pretoria
South Africa

First Edition 2009

ISBN: 978-1-875093-77-9

BRIZA

website: www.briza.co.za

Design and layout: Hendali Steynberg
Copy-editor: Francis Perrier
Proofreader: Tanya Mcleod
Printed and bound by Craft Print International Ltd, Singapore

Dedicated to my many students everywhere,
who have - or will one day - become home owners too.
I hope the thrill of designing never dies
and your own gardens become true expressions of who you are
and what you want your space to be.

CONTENTS

'The time has come,' the Walrus said,

'To talk of many things:

Of shoes – and ships – and sealing-wax –

Of cabbages – and kings'

Lewis Carroll

'Through the Looking Glass'
(1872)

FOREWORD

Anywhere in the world where people have experienced the thrill of watching a garden develop from a bare patch of ground over a period of time, you will find people exuding a kind of smugness when they talk of their 'home-n-garden' – and quite rightly so. There is nothing quite as satisfying as the feeling gardeners have when they hesitantly approach a new patch of land, a garden space in a new city, climate zone or a larger or smaller space, with the knowledge that they know just how to go about designing their new space. Not only are they able to include all their garden fantasies – well, a good few of them at least, they are also able to visualise how it will look a few years down the line and avoid costly time-consuming mistakes.

How do they do it, you ask. Quite simply by getting to know the 'building-blocks' needed to provide the ideal garden – then there is little left to chance as plants are chosen or disregarded, paving materials considered, or pros and cons of a pool, pond or play-pit for the kids. Time is a-wasting when you need firm choices for the ideal garden, and soon runs out if too much hesitation is encountered. They want the lush lawn, bright seasonal colour and a place for the dog to run – and dig if need be – and they want is as soon as possible ... and the answer to creating that small piece of Utopia is careful planning.

The last thing I would want to commit myself to would be the re-invention of the landscape design wheel. However, I have been asked so many times to write an easy-to-understand, no-frills book to help with designing the average home garden, and now seemed as good a time as any to start.

Sorry, control freaks – there are no rules and regulations! This is not a step-by-step guide to perfection in design (if such an aspect does exist in landscape design I would personally love to know more about it). It simply sets out ideas, guidelines and suggestions that will result in you, the home owner, creating a successful garden to fit your needs and expectations.

All sites have design pitfalls and problem areas. As you work your way through the following pages you will pick up on the warning signs, reroute your thinking and avoid costly and time-consuming mistakes.

Over the years I have realised that landscape designing is not simply a question of using the right plants in the right places. Not all instances in a garden call for plants – and not all tricky situations can be solved by using plants – so hard landscape elements (known as HLE) such as paving, screening and other non-plant items, need to be included. I have done so, and included some handy tips on installation and selection.

'Even if I knew that tomorrow the world would go to pieces, I would still plant my apple tree'

Martin Luther

German religious reformist
(1483–1546)

As a home owner, you want your property to be unique in one way or another. There are chapters on how to include features such as water, containers, ornamentation and wildlife in the design, as well as ideas on how standard 'off-the-shelf' items can be incorporated into specific, personalised landscapes.

Because gardens are not static and cast in stone, there is a chapter on redesigning and revamping old or unsuccessful parts of a garden. This is an all-too-important aspect of gardening, especially for people buying older homes, building-on to existing homes or upgrading any part of a garden that has not quite come up to expectations.

No written guide to landscape designing for the home owner would be worth much if it didn't include some mention of costing and calculation, so without dating the book to a specific era, I have included a chapter on how to calculate quantities and costs of some of the more used materials and in some cases I have suggested effective alternatives.

The idea behind writing this book is not to help people design gardens like I do, or in fact like anybody else does. I hope to encourage interested gardeners to realise that they can create a well-designed garden – one that will see to their needs, relevant to their particular set of conditions and circumstances, financial or otherwise – and that they will have a fair idea of why they designed it the way they did.

I don't for one minute regard this book as the 'be-all and end-all' of all things to do with landscape designing, but I trust that anyone using it will have fun doing so. At the same time, I hope that aspirant designers will learn design confidence from it, which will allow them to enter the wonderful world of personal garden design experimentation with true enjoyment, confidence and a sense of exuberant vigour, regardless of the result.

Lynton Johnson

A well-designed shrubbery will provide the vista and the privacy all too often needed in an urban garden.

TO BEGIN WITH...

Like any other important journey, a trip into the realm of landscape design starts with some kind of idea of direction and an awareness of obvious landmarks.

To provide some of that initial confidence, let me start off by saying that there is no great mystery about designing a garden. Anybody with an awareness of what they want to have happen on the open space surrounding a home (or any other fixed structure), can, if guided by common sense and some basic design and plant facts, put together a setting in which they are happy – well, with regard to the outcome of the garden at least!

I would suggest a critical walk around the property to start things off properly – and *critical* is the key factor. Make a list of all the obvious aspects that will impact on a design.

Services

These are those oft-hidden mod cons that make suburban life bearable:

*   sewer lines, septic tanks, soak pits, submerged storm water systems (as opposed to the water rushing across the surface)
*   electrical cables, water mains and meter boxes, as well as the taps or valves which turn the water on or off
*   gas lines in some areas
*   telephone lines – more relevant in complexes, otherwise they are generally above ground, but still need to be listed
*   municipal servitudes, which are areas you own but can't do too much with, because they are reserved for the extension of general services within most residential areas. (Servitudes can, in most cases, be identified on any municipal development or urban street maps.)

Don't ignore anything that would have an impact beyond your control. This includes overhead power networks, and long-term developments such as major road systems and new housing developments.

chapter 1

In some cases, the view, albeit man-made is as pleasant enough to live with as any natural wonder.

Surroundings

A less-than-pleasing outlook is not so serious when viewed from areas like the kitchen service area, the bathroom or garage, but its importance will be magnified if a cluttered view of urban lifestyles happens to be most of what is seen from the lounge, patio or outdoor entertainment area.

Only the farming community and large land-owners are blessed with a feeling of total space – the rest of us have to create it. Almost all homes are surrounded at reasonably close quarters by other developments. Their occupants generally desire the same things as we do – privacy and a beautiful living space. Look around and note who and what borders onto your space. For a fortunate few there will be pleasant vistas out over hills, valleys, mountains, rivers, and the sea, with all the romantic feeling of space this encourages. For others, the outlook will include shopping complexes, multi-storey buildings, railway lines, motorways, and so on – the variations on this theme are numerous. What the latter all have in common is that we would rather be less aware of them. To allow this to happen, they have to be identified and noted first.

Consider what level of privacy you have and whether it is sufficient, permanent and durable. If the neighbour's garden provides your privacy, you could be badly affected when they decide to redevelop their property, ending up with little or no privacy as a result.

Climate

One thing we're all aware of while it's happening is weather. However, strangely enough, it's the first thing forgotten when buying plants, especially those that are a little more specific in their climatic requirements. If there is to be any hope of creating a satisfactory design, the critical role of the weather will have to be taken into account. The most important aspects to note are the following:

- Seasonal change in the position of *sun and shade* areas. The plants used in these areas need to be able to tolerate annual changes – more sun for some months or more shade – either will have an impact on how these plants grow.

- The *rainfall pattern* – how much rain can be expected, at what times of the year, and in what forms – hail, cloudbursts and violent storms, or soft and penetrating rainfall. This will indicate what forms of canopy cover, if any, are needed to make certain aspects of the garden more usable. It will also indicate what methods will need to be incorporated in the design to accommodate water during the rainy season.

- The rise and fall of *temperature* during the various seasons and times of day and night, as well as the micro-climates created by open spaces between buildings. Structures such as walls, or areas protected by established plants, are critical to the ideal growing conditions of your chosen plants. They will also allow a range of plants – from tender, frost-sensitive impatiens to cactuses – to be incorporated in the same garden space. Being aware of temperature fluctuations will also allow you to allocate garden areas to the most sensible uses, such as a warm area for a patio generally used in winter when other areas of the garden are too cold.

- The impact that *winter weather* will have on the garden. The word 'frost' often sends hesitant gardeners into a complete state of panic as the winter season draws nearer. Little do they realise just what a vast range of frost-tolerant plant material is available! Matching these hardy plants to your 'cold garden' options can provide many interesting design challenges.

- Whether a gentle breeze on a sweltering summer's day, or the gale forces which lash some parts of the country from time to time, *wind* is an important aspect of climatic behaviour because of the damage it can cause to plants and structures alike. It is important to realise that it is not only within the confines of your own garden space that the wind patterns should be noted; the prevailing winds are also a force to be reckoned with within the area at large. Take note of any specific wind trends, such as could be experienced at the coast, in the Cape, or below the Drakensberg, as well as the dry dust storm-prone areas – they will make gardening more of a challenge than some folk are prepared for (and nothing discourages the intrepid new gardener more than being caught off-balance by the elements).

Top left: Only a select few home owners are privileged to have a vista that is a sheer delight to live with.

Top: Sometimes a limited planting can provide all the privacy that a specific area in the garden requires.

Middle: A lush semi-tropical palm garden won't grow everywhere but with careful planning similar effects can be obtained in time with careful plant selection.

Bottom: This quiet, simple uncluttered entrance to a home implies 'Welcome, come in and relax and forget the busy outside world'.

Hardy Euphorbia *species may be the ideal screening material in dry areas where watering is problematic.*

On an undeveloped property, check which direction the prevalent winds come from – they could influence where outdoor recreation areas such as a swimming pool, spa or semi-covered entertainment area will be situated, and whether solid screening structures will need to be incorporated as part of your final design or not. Remember that screening for privacy and screening against unfavourable weather conditions can go hand in hand when considering these aspects of your design.

If you are new to an area, it is a good idea to ask long-term residents what you should expect in the way of wind, rain and winter conditions, so that you can design your open spaces with some form of awareness, protection and control in mind.

The site

Obviously you need to assess your particular site – after all, when it comes down to reality this is the area that you intend to design for visual as well as practical, usable purposes. If the area has already been prepared and planted – in other words, it is not a new, undeveloped site – take time to weigh up all that happens in this garden during the coming seasons and months. The existing plant material may offer some pleasing surprises, or some may disappoint you. In some cases, unknown plants may provide interest as the seasons change. I tend to suggest the simple 'wait and see' tactic rather than blindly rushing in and making changes, only to realise all too late that you could have saved money or time with a little patience.

Above: It is important to asses all that is on a property prior to making dramatic changes. Here is a well-developed clump of indigenous ilala palm – Hyphaene sp. *which should be kept intact.*

Right: Detail design work to look out onto makes the home owner less aware of the high boundary walls beyond the planting.

During your period of tentative observation, keep a keen eye on how the rain pattern behaves and how it moves through your new garden space. Does it tend to wash areas away, dam up in other areas or move readily through the garden away from the house and swimming pool and exit the property in an acceptable manner? Does it soak into the soil easily, or take days to soak away? Will you need to change the soil texture to encourage drainage, and if so to what extent? Will trenches filled with gravel and stone under the final soil level, known as French drains, be the answer? Will simple soil reshaping suffice to get the water to move in an ideal direction? Simply bearing all this in mind will help you make wise plant choices at a later stage.

In some areas the soil tends to expand or contract depending on the moisture and clay content of the soil (wet or dry seasons), and this can play havoc with paved areas and structures such as tennis courts, swimming pools and fish ponds. If the garden should be in such an area, I suggest that any major developments or changes to the garden design are first discussed with the necessary experts such as civil engineers, perhaps geologists, or at least a few well-chosen experienced local landscape contractors.

Although I am suggesting a period of observation in semi-established gardens, there is no harm in carefully assessing all relevant factors on any site, prior to initiating your design. Pay attention to the structure of your soil, which can be upgraded, improved and kept healthy with good standard horticultural practices such as regular composting. On the other hand, if there are large rock outcrops, shallow soil areas with underlying rock, if the soil is of an undesirable colour or the property slopes in the 'wrong' direction, these are all unchangeable aspects of the terrain, which have to be included into the overall landscape design of the area. Logically there is not much that can be done about changing these realities, but knowing about them will prove invaluable when looking for ideal positions for future structural items such as pools, ponds, gazebos and the like – it can even make digging a tree hole easier!

At this early stage in any area to be designed, it is a good idea to view the outdoor areas from indoors. Looking through doors and windows helps to 'box' or frame some views and vistas and enables the viewer to see them as they will day after day when inside the building. This often helps to pinpoint areas that when seen as a general part of the garden seem easy to deal with, but seen from a specific indoor position often take on an important or challenging role, which may call for specific design attention (see Chapter 5).

It's important to see the *whole* site as being part of the design scheme, including the less favourable, yet important areas such as any service or parking areas, pathways and driveways as well as general outdoor storage areas that may be deemed necessary, like compost or general bulk refuse sites. A good working design will successfully include such areas without detracting from the overall design. Please remember that such 'everyday' areas need to be designed as part of the overall concept rather than 'squeezed in' somewhere in the back yard.

Specific rooms call for specific attention when planning outside their windows or doors.

Above: Simple plant repetition always has a dramatic impact.

Top: For the elderly a collection of interesting containers at a raised level makes life easier.

Middle: Consider the small detailed areas and include them into the bigger scheme of things.

Bottom: Well chosen accessories help to add to the intended atmosphere or mood of any area.

Right: Décor in any 'room' is important – here lemon yellow is ideal as a form of colour for a summer garden – With a touch of orange Crocosmia to brighten things up.

It is very important that you constantly relate the smaller, detailed areas within the site to the larger overall picture. Should you fail to do this you could easily land up with an unrelated 'patchwork' of ideas and a very disjointed design.

The needs of individuals

Perhaps the most important element of the proposed design is that Mr and Mrs Happy Home owner, the persons who create the design, *use* the outdoor space as readily and as regularly as their inside spaces. After all, the garden is also composed of rooms with alternative walls, floors and ceilings!

Needless to say, there must be some element of discussion and planning among the people who will interact with the area or areas designed. It is not uncommon for the dominant garden lover to prescribe to other users how things are going to be – and if there is no opposition to this approach, at the design stage, all is well and good. However, it does tend to result in the site being created in a manner favoured by one soul to the frustrating exclusion of all other users' needs or preferences. To reduce the likelihood of a blood feud among the parties involved, it is an idea to consider all possible requests, current and intended.

Consider the ages of the users, not that people will necessarily stay in one home for their entire lives, but simply because there are going to be subconscious demands from various age groups all the time.

- Baby – a shady area for a pram: make sure that it is visible from the main areas of activity in and outside the house.

- Toddler – a hard surface to play on with push cars and bicycles, making sure that the area can be seen easily and that it is away from ponds and swimming pools.

- Six- to ten-year-olds – climbing equipment (or where possible encourage tree climbing – perhaps build a tree house!) Consider a sand pit and an area that the kids feel is their own. You might even encourage the development of their own garden where some easy plants can be grown.

- Teenagers – an area for physical forms of recreation as well as somewhere sunny to relax: consider the adolescent need for privacy.

- The adult home owner – an entertainment area as well as areas of specific activity – vegetable garden, glasshouse, other plant collections, and sport facilities.

- The elderly – quiet, shady areas away from the more frantic family activities. Raised planting areas will encourage those for whom bending is a problem to keep their green thumb active.

Consider areas for the family pets – gardening with curious dogs can often be an expensive challenge.

If the garden or outdoor areas are to be developed in phases, earmark the position of major items that will come later. These are generally costly items that will have a decided impact on the existing garden – such as pool, water feature, tennis court, or perhaps a garden cottage. Being constantly aware of their intended position reduces the temptation to do a little something in these areas in the short-term; this save time and money in the long run.

On a more detailed level, plant preferences, favoured colours, shapes and styles can be listed. These listings make it easier to please other users as well as help keep track of plants and things while trying to pull the whole overall picture together.

The whole picture

The overall site is one that consists of open spaces as well as fixed structures and facilities. In most cases, somebody who had no idea of anybody's garden and/or outdoor preferences has designed these buildings with some architectural style or appearance in mind, and the home owner-cum-designer needs to combine the two parts into a whole liveable concept. To do this effectively, give attention to the style or overall appearance of the building structure included in the area to be landscaped. By doing this it is possible to avoid creating a landscape design that is in conflict with the structure's appearance –

Top: Make sure that a patio is not simply attractive but large enough to accommodate people AND furnishings.

Middle: Providing all the recreational space and activities for children in one area means simplified supervision

Bottom: A slightly more private area for the older children will surely be appreciated – by everyone!

Above left and right: Consider the architecture as part of the overall design and not simply a backdrop to the plants.

or worse, doesn't visually include buildings at all. It can safely be said that time is not wasted by carefully planning the early stages of the process – after all, it's all part of a cost-free process, which will save time and money further down the line.

A scrapbook (or several) of pictures and ideas may help develop a clearer concept of what design direction the designer intends heading in and often offers clarity because one can see what is intended. I carry notebooks with me and constantly make notes or sketch odd images as they come to the 'grey filing cabinet' – unusual colour or plant combinations, the use of an unusual product or simply a novel idea, for example, but more of this aspect in Chapter 3.

Don't be scared to be bold when using accessories – especially if space allows – but don't over-crowd.

More will be said regarding style (Chapter 8) at a later stage, but it is important that first-time garden designers learn to regard structures as equally important as other fixed elements such as weather and the seasons.

So much for the early stages: a general, overall awareness of when and how the design will start to take place is now firmly fixed in the designer's mind.

MEASURING UP

In all designs, there is a direct relationship between accuracy and the success and cost-effectiveness of the project or item – and garden design is no different. Although scale relates to several different aspects of landscape design (these will be dealt with as the need arises), at this stage the only aspect that needs to be considered is that of simple metres and centimetres – in other words, measuring distances on the site and conveying these measurements (in a usable, reduced scale) to paper for the purposes of accurate planning.

Site plan

Measuring the area will provide some simple answers to questions that often go unasked: for example, will the patio furniture fit into the area intended for a patio? Don't guess – measure the area and draw your own conclusions – either enlarge the patio if space allows or simply buy a smaller set of furniture. I told you it was all basic!

Above: Either enlarge the patio or simply buy a smaller set of furniture.

The easiest way to work to scale is to measure in metres and centimetres, reduce to centimetres and millimetres, and convey the dimensions to paper. Commonly, a metre in reality (on the ground) is portrayed as one centimetre on paper. This scale is referred to as 1:100, the design being accurate but one hundred times smaller than reality. To make life even easier, graph paper divided into centimetres and millimetres can be purchased: it's simply a question of placing the relevant information in the correct places on the graph paper. Still only basic, easy things to do!

The task of transferring your home onto paper will be greatly simplified if building plans are available, either from developers, architects, and building contractors, or in the case of older homes, from the local authorities. In some of the pre-metric

era designs these plans are probably in feet and inches, in which case it's a good idea to employ the assistance of someone who knows how to convert these measurements to a metric scale. However it's not that difficult, if you have an old imperial scale rule and the scale is known or indicated on the plans (they will either be $1/16^{th}$ inch to the foot or $1/8^{th}$ inch to the foot), measure with the old rule, count the number of sixteenths or eighths (which will be the number of feet) and using a calculator times the number of feet by 2,50 – and voila, you have the measurement in centimetres.

In some cases, particularly with older homes, non-residential structures such as summer houses, extra garages, storerooms and even staff quarters or garden cottages were often built without proper plans being drawn up. Generally this means that before attempting any landscape planning, you will have to do some detailed measuring up, simply to position these structures reasonably accurately within the parameters of the site. If you are in this tedious position I offer a few pointers.

- Any plans that indicate the size, proportions and measurements of the general site (including boundaries, fences, entrances from roads) will be of value – even if they have to be redrawn by a draftsman. For the more adventurous garden designer, you could look for plans that indicate other aspects too, such as contour lines – indicating land height, steep and gradual slopes – and for the fortunate, rivers are usually indicated as well. These plans, generally ideal for indicating large sites such as whole suburbs, farms and small agricultural sites rather than specific urban properties, are accurately measured by surveyors and are available from the Government Printer.

- Measure each of the individual structures separately – if in doubt of getting bogged down with measuring all the various structures, their sizes and their distance and positions one to another, use separate sheets of metric graph paper – this is a simple way of avoiding confusion – as long as each structure is measured using the same scale as the others and each measured item is identified with a name or description, e.g. 'large tree near tap' or 'main house', garden cottages, and so on.

- I suggest that you work on the 1:100 scale: one centimetre equals a metre, five millimetres equals a half metre and one millimetre equals ten centimetres. This is relatively simple to grasp with a bit of practice and relates to most measurable items in garden design.

- Once the structures have been measured, measure the distance between them and their positions relevant to the boundaries or other fixed items. A simple system known as 'triangulation' may be used as a means of doing this.

  Triangulation is a calculation that enables you to fix a third point (such as a tree, the corner of an adjacent building or corner post of a property), when two other fixed points (such as house corners or property corners) are known.

In small areas a smaller seating area – well planned – has more impact and is more acceptable.

First, measure the distance between the two fixed points, convert the measurement to the scale intended, and convey this measurement to the graph paper plan.

Next, measure the distance to the third item or position from both of the two fixed points, and with the help of a pair of compasses, plot these measurements on the plan.

The position of the third item is where the two to-scale drawn arcs cross.

Once the third position has been plotted it in turn can be used as one of the fixed points from which further items or positions can be measured.

Once you have measured each structure and the distances between them as well as their position in relation to boundaries and other fixed items such as trees or paved areas – in fact anything that will be retained and included in your proposed design, stick all your various pieces of paper together (if you measured each item separately), place another piece of paper over these and trace all the measured components onto one plan. This is known as a site plan.

Finally, all the existing services noted in the initial survey of the property can be added, as accurately as is possible when trying to position things that are buried underground!

This is understandably a rather tedious task, but if planned carefully and with a reasonable level of accuracy it's generally a 'once-off' project and the resultant site plan can be used as a base from which other fixed structural planning as well as landscape planning can be developed.

Left, right and round-about

I mentioned at the beginning of this section that there were other aspects of scale that would prove to be important as the design began to take shape. For example, don't be led into believing that design has to be all about straight lines and square corners – not at all. Circles, curves, angles and triangles can be incorporated along with the lines and corners to create a feeling of movement.

Curves are often created by using a warm, pliable hosepipe at the whim of the home owner. In many cases these appear as a series of bites and squiggles surrounding the lawn. Because there are no specific rules and methods to create appealing curves in a design, this aspect will be dealt with at a later stage (see Chapter 8). For now, a few simple pointers will suffice to create perfect squares, triangles and circles for wherever they are needed.

Making a circle. Vehicle turning-circle, pond, lawn area or patio? The size of a circle or part circle is determined by the distance from the centre point to the edge, called the radius. On paper, using a pair of compasses, determine the size of the circle and the position of the centre point – obviously this is relevant to what the circle is intended to represent; a vehicle turning circle; pond; lawn area or patio. Remember realistic-scale of such items as turning circles. Having positioned the circle in a design or in relation to other structures, measure the position of the centre in relation to other fixed items (this is where triangulation helps) and the length of the radius, and knock in a peg. Using a length of string that does not stretch, tie one end loosely to this peg, making sure that it can pivot. Attach the other end of the string to another peg so that the distance between the two pegs is equal to the radius of the circle. Draw the circle on the ground, making sure that the string is taut and that the centre peg is not pulled over. Retain the centre peg and the string until all work regarding the circle has been completed.

Making a triangle. For triangles of irregular shapes, use the triangulation method, relying on two fixed points and measuring the sides of the triangle to the third point. For a right-angled triangle (where one corner is 90 degrees – square, in other words), there are two methods. With triangulation, measure one side of the triangle 5 metres long. The other two sides must be 4 and 3 metres respectively. The corner between the 3 and 4 metre sides will be 90 degrees square.

The second method requires a length of string with markings at 3 metres, 4 metres and finally at 5 metres distance (the string's total length will be 12 metres). Join the two ends of the string and firmly stretch the three marked positions away from each other – the resulting triangle will be a right-angled triangle with the square corner between the 3 and 4 metre markings.

A square or oblong. Create one square corner as indicated above and extend or reduce the two sides' lengths as required. Then from these two points attach a length of string equal in length to the sum of the two sides (mark their lengths) and pull the string taut at the joining point of the two lengths. This is the fourth corner and all four corners will be square.

Obviously where and when these shapes will be applied will be determined by the final style in which the design is drawn, which will get further mention in Chapter 8 under the heading 'Styles'.

Attempt where possible to keep curves simple and easy flowing.

Opposite page

Top: Simple straight lines are often the most dramatic in limited space.

Bottom: Allow beds to curve easily and without excessive detail through the space allowed.

Above: Remember the practical uses of such elements as bridges – people must be able to use them with ease.

Below

Left: Allow workable space around planted areas if the need arises – in this case from the house to an outdoor living area.

Middle: Don't make paved areas outside living areas too small – the bigger the better.

Right: Practical sized areas around such facilities as swimming pools where there is a chance of reasonable activity adds to the safety of the area whilst keeping it visually balanced and to scale.

Realistic measurements

Simply put, this form of measuring relates to items that must have a realistic size in order to be practical. For example, chairs and tables are built to standard heights so that the users may be able to comfortably relate to them as functional items. Many items within any designed garden space have practical measurements, and if these all-important metres and centimetres are ignored then the particular element, when included in your design, will probably not fulfil its intended function. It sounds too technical to be fun, but as is often the case, many of these items are taken for granted, only to jar when they are wrongly designed or installed.

A few practical examples are steps, pathways, driveways, patio areas, summer house type situations (I refuse to call every outdoor structure a 'lapa'), even swimming pool sizes, parking areas, utility or working spaces and simple dimensions such as the width of anywhere required for more than one person to walk and not feel crowded! Not to mention facilities for frail or wheelchair-bound persons (in such cases it is wise to consult doctors or other specialists as to what dimension, gradients and turning or mounting/dismounting spaces are required).

Most of these measurements are evaluated simply by observation, but where people tend to make mistakes is to take such everyday

measurements for granted and to create the proposed heights, widths or areas without careful consideration. Then, when it's costly to repair, rebuild or begin again, they realise the error of their ways!

Below are some simple guidelines.

Pathways

For comfortable use of a pathway, where there is very little likelihood that more than one person will use it at any one time – such as a service pathway through flowerbeds or vegetable, rose or herb gardens – a reasonably narrow pathway can be created. This could be as narrow as 30 cm but generally for easy use stick to a minimum of 50 cm. If this pathway is to be built using paving slabs, use either a single row of 50 cm square slabs or any slab combination that creates a similar width pathway. If the same areas are to accommodate a wheelbarrow or lawnmower to and from the tool shed, compost heap or store room, I would suggest that the path should be at least a metre wide, or two 50 cm paving slabs side by side (three 30 cm slabs would also work). If either of these two pathways are made with bricks the narrow path would have either 3 or 5 rows of bricks and the wider one 5 to 10 rows of bricks depending on whether the bricks are used with their width or length side by side. Obviously if gravel, pebbles, ash or any other loose material is used for pathways a practical minimum width would still be 50 cm, but there is no limit to the final width. Ensure that the loose material is contained within some form of immovable edge, which is firmly embedded into the ground – this is generally known as a kerb, header-course or mowing edge.

When constructing or designing a pathway that slopes it is important to consider its gradient (the steepness of the area between two points). If the area is too steep then the need for steps becomes important; on the other hand, if it's possible to avoid steps in areas where the elderly are to walk then a gradual meandering pathway with hand rails could be a better idea.

In the case of very steep properties this is an important aspect when positioning the house with regard to access for vehicles as well as pedestrians. Perhaps the services of a surveyor will be needed to determine the ideal route for the driveway and establishing the gradients of such a driveway. Regular replacement of a car's clutch can prove to be a costly process!

If the path is to serve as a walkway for more than one person, such as most

Top: A simple yet practical path of random slate meanders through a shrubbery too wide for easy maintenance.

Below left: Where traffic and pedestrians are to share roads make sure that the facilities are wide enough for both at the same time.

Below right: In narrow areas, narrow, yet practical pathways make for easy access from one area to another. Note 'lifting' of some planting to reduce crowding as the plants mature.

A practical yet attractive driveway adds interest to the entrance of any home.

entrances, links between buildings and larger public arrival points such as plaza pick-up points for transport and other areas where there is a constant flow of people, the minimum width would be 1200 mm and this would increase to 3-5 metres depending on the amount of pedestrian traffic.

Driveways and vehicle parking areas

In the average domestic situation driveways are intended to accommodate lightweight vehicles rather than extreme heavy duty vehicles, so turning circles, parking spaces and road widths are much less than in commercial and industrial situations. But it's surprising just how many people who own vehicles forget how much space they take up when they design parking areas.

Generally a 3-metre wide driveway will suffice unless there is a constant flow of cars and similar sized vehicles in both directions, such as one would find in housing complexes, school, church and sport club parking areas, in which case 5-6 metres width would be better. Parking for a single car is 2,5 metres wide and a minimum of 5 metres in length and a comfortable area to turn in is based on a turning curve with a 5-metre radius. Bigger vehicles should be carefully planned for before any other elements of the design are considered (this is a situation often encountered when the designer has to plan a farm or smallholding garden).

Drive-through, circular or crescent driveways are less popular today, probably as a result of smaller properties; however if you should find yourself contemplating such a driveway make sure to incorporate a pull-off parking area for cars, otherwise you could find cars park one behind the other and everybody has to wait for the first arrival to leave first and so on down the line. Very frustrating!

As a last word on parking allocation – since it is almost impossible to determine the amount of parking required in a garden and to allow for the overflow, it is not a bad idea to incorporate some open lawn areas (depending on the design, these areas could also be paved or covered with gravel), which are generally simple open aspects of the design, perhaps accommodating a tree or two. As this does not happen too often, the lawn will not be too affected – and the vehicles will be kept off the streets. Alternatively, if pavement width allows, parking can be accommodated in the simple design of this area.

Patio, sun deck, 'lapa' and other solid surface entertainment areas

These may vary quite wildly, because each one has to cater to individual requirements. In other words, no two spaces are the same. Be this as it may, there are still measurement requirements that are too often overlooked. The first horrendous mistake people make when considering the size of their built outdoor space is that it not only has to accommodate people, but also the furniture that that the users will sit on or at. Tables, chairs, benches, even log stumps, bales of straw or bean bags take up space and if the area is intended to comfortably accommodate a number of visitors, there has to be a similar amount of space allocated to the furniture as well as space to walk to and between them.

Even the simple task of installing a garden bench among the shrubberies as well as having access to it means that scale of space and item needs to be considered.

An acceptable rule of thumb when providing standing space for people would be to provide at least one square metre per person. This could include the chair or any other form of single seating, but would not include the table and pedestrian traffic space to and from the site.

Steps and walls

In most sites that are not altogether level, or with a gradient too steep for a casual meandering pathway, the need for steps may arise. Although the formal levelled terrace garden is no longer that popular, there are still areas in any property which are more functional if levelled off to some extent. Into the home, out into the rest of the site, or from one levelled area of the garden to another – all may require a step or two.

The standard height of a step 'riser' should not exceed 200 mm; for casual climbing 150 mm is ideal. The width of each step tread should be at least 300 mm, but wider steps can be used. Too wide a step tread is uncomfortable to climb, however. If the steps are created out of railway sleepers, natural rock pieces or stacked bank-retaining blocks and are intended for casual access to parts of the garden, the height of the riser and width of tread are less important and usually determined by the material used.

To begin with, where the slope is slight and only a few steps are needed, it is wise to vertically excavate a section of the slope to determine how many steps will be required prior to setting out to build them. If you intend to build the steps yourself, start with a proper foundation, good-quality building material and sound advice from someone who knows how to go about it. Remember that any structure should be created to last indefinitely and not fall apart, sink, or subside in a short while.

An important aspect when designing steps from or to an area is that disabled users who are dependent on a wheelchair may visit the area. Should this be the case, the desired ramp and pathways should be built to the required measurements. It may be necessary to call in the help of professional designers to advise on such aspects.

Top: In a reasonably small area a railway sleeper 'wall' cleanly defines the raised 'sundeck' in this beautifully geometric design.

Middle: A low retaining walled planter elevate some 'fantasy' pruned Duranta 'Sheena's Gold' *shrubs to level with the patio area.*

Bottom: Pools and ponds are generally designed to enhance and fit into a specific space for a particular visual effect, rather than to comply with enormous 'Olympic' proportions.

Although steps can be a casual means of moving from one level to another in a garden and can, in some cases, be more for visual than totally functional effects, walls generally have functional purposes and being costly items should be well built to serve their specific functions.

Whether the walls are designed to create privacy, retain soil, provide work or seating surfaces or serve as raised planting areas or ponds, there are dimensions that have to be considered if the construction is to be functional. Low walls of less than 1200 mm in height can be built of a single brick width (100 mm thick), with few or no supporting pillars. This would be ideal for low planter boxes, small fish ponds, a seat or table support or a wall to demarcate or enclose an area within the garden. Boundary walls and walls taller than 1200 mm have to be built at least two bricks thick (210 mm thick), with supporting columns approximately every 3 metres apart, and wire 'brick force' is often employed between the layers to add extra strength. Walls that are intended to retain soil, hold back banks and support heavy overhead structures should be designed by a civil engineer to avoid any serious mishaps in the future. One important aspect to be considered with such walls is that water in the soil can build up tremendous pressure on them from behind: if poorly built with insufficient or badly placed drainage they may fall over!

Pools and ponds

Although ponds are generally designed to fit the space and funding available, there are some fundamental aspects of scale that need to be considered. One of the simplest mistakes made when building these items is that the initial shape and depth or width are often calculated without taking the building materials into account and when completed are too deep, too shallow or too small. When excavating (in fact from the design stage), make sure that the thickness of the materials to be used for construction is taken into account. If streams move from one pond to another, make sure that they are deep and wide enough to carry the volume of water intended. Keep the edges of ponds as unobtrusive as possible by thinning them down as they reach ground level, to avoid thick unsightly cement rims around the feature.

Make sure that the concrete casting of informal free-flow ponds is thick enough not to crack with time – at least 75 mm thick, and if the size exceeds 1500 mm in any direction, it would be wise to incorporate wire mesh reinforcing in the concrete. This is particularly important in areas where the soil has a high clay content and shrinks and expands as the wet and dry seasons come and go. Insufficient reinforcing will result in the structure cracking.

If a swimming pool is to be designed, keep the pool proportionate to the area, with sufficient surround space for the users to walk, sit or lie on. Avoid large, deep pools – they are costly to run and can take ages to warm up after winter. Provide a reasonable area for 'playing', even avoiding a deep-end altogether. Make sure that children can easily get in and out of the pool by providing enough manageable steps.

Although there are no specific dimensions for fishponds, water features or swimming pools, any or all of these elements should appear to be in proportion to the area into which they are incorporated, becoming part of the design rather than dominating it. Should there be doubt or hesitation, there are numerous competent experts to ask.

Home-based sports facilities

Many children dream of having their own personal soccer, rugby or cricket pitch at home. With the current trend towards smaller properties this is pretty certain to remain a dream, but yet there are some sport facilities, which need specific sizes and if space allows they can be included in the garden. A basket ball ring is set 3 metres high, a lawn area 20 × 10 metres will accommodate volleyball and several other ball games and a tennis court would require an area of 18 × 36 metres in length, (although there are slightly smaller courts and ball-wall, or practice wall dimensions too). Obviously to make the game fair for all who play, it is advisable that the area should be as correct and level as possible.

Storage facilities

Whether this takes on the form of a wooden, prefabricated hut or a properly constructed brick storeroom or tool shed, it is important to remember that the facility will need some approach and work space outside, which will be as important as the space inside. If a ladder, wheelbarrow, garden tools and lawnmower are to be stored, the chances are the standard 3 x 3 metre hut will hardly be big enough. And if the structure is squashed between the house and boundary wall there will be so little space outside it to work in – cleaning the lawnmower, for example – that the storage facility will become a neglected place for broken things. Whatever the floor space is inside the storage facility, make sure that there is a similar level area designed outside it to serve as a hobby area or general work space.

Shrubberies

Deciding how wide or how long these areas should be, is like wondering just how high clouds are or how 'long is a piece of string?' There are no hard or fast rules for shrubberies, but there are logical guidelines that make planting areas easier to manage and grow plants in. Generally beds are created to grow plants *and* also to serve some form of alternative function. Much of this alternative function is related to screening and privacy on or near boundaries. Generally there is space here, yet there is a general tendency to keep these beds narrow, yet filled with plant material, which is intended to help block off parts of the outside world.

Top: An elegant cluster of water jets periodically break the surface of this shallow, yet beautifully simple water feature.

Above: Water in ponds often allows for interesting surface detail – generally without extreme depth.

Below: Often space only allows for a single dramatic jet of water to add movement to the area.

Above: An impractically narrow bed along a pathway generally serves little or no purpose and perhaps the grass should have been allowed to grow to the pathway instead.

Top: A simple yet dramatic planting easily sets the right atmosphere in any garden space.

Above left: A newly planted shrubbery in proportion to the area – this planting will in time easily screen the neighbouring buildings.

Often this results in the plants overgrowing the beds and killing off the grass or encroaching on paths and driveways.

Boundary beds or shrubberies should not be narrower than 1 metre, and unless pathways are included, not wider than 3 metres (see 'The purpose of Plants' – Chapter 7). In narrow areas where a pedestrian link and privacy are required – perhaps between the house or other fixed structures and the boundaries – select upright growing plant material, consider a wall rather than plants to screen, and if plants are intended, reduce the pathway to a practical minimum. Containers in such a situation are often a solution.

Free-standing or free-form beds within the lawn area can be wider because maintenance can be applied from all sides and the wider, taller plants can be included in the inner areas. The length of these beds is seldom relevant except where there is a need or tendency to pass through them from one area to another, in which case provide logical pathways at the required positions, to serve the specific needs. Stepping stones, lawn, paving or gravel may be ideal solutions, depending on the particular uses (moving a lawnmower from one area to another; providing access to a tap, electrical control point or post box; pulling a hosepipe or pushing a wheelbarrow, and so on).

If these measurements are given due consideration early in the design phase, if the necessary experts are consulted where necessary and proper provision made to incorporate good design principles correctly and logically into the plan, they will automatically become integral parts of the design. This is what gives a property a feeling of balance and total involvement of all the components, however large, important, small or incidental.

Above far left: This planting however will gradually outgrow the width of the planting area causing the grass to die off.

Above middle left: A wide planting calls for a pathway though it for practical maintenance purposes.

Above middle right: In areas where there is little need for wide pathways and space is limited keep the paths, plantings and plant choices to practical proportions.

Above far right: Planted containers in very narrow areas are a perfect alternative to designing any plant-beds at all.

IN THE MOOD

There is a tendency today to open gardens to the public for the purpose of fundraising for one charitable institution or another. The interested visitors often have another motive in mind, namely a little light pilfering, not in the physical sense, but visually. They go to get new and stimulating ideas.

Deciding on how a garden is to be designed is perhaps the hardest part of all. Often there are dozens of fragmented ideas to draw from, and yet the intention is that the garden should end up being in harmony with the home, its owners and their needs and likes as well as aspirations for their garden's future development.

Not all potential home owners are able to see clearly, let alone create, their dream garden. They need a little extra inspiration. To help solve this quandary I suggest compiling a **mood board**.

A mood board is simply a means of taking the obvious and the intended and compiling a visual collection of these in such a way that they look and feel right together. In the same way as paint charts are collected and combined to select the ideal colour and textured finish combinations for a home, or material samples are collected to ensure the right 'look' for an interior design, so the mood board helps pull garden components and ideas together.

Remember that the home is of a specific size and style and fits onto a specific shape and size of property. These are basic visual facts. Everything after this is at the whim and fancy of the home owner. Start by collecting ideas, pictures or photos of gardens or sections of gardens that appeal, and soon a specific tendency or preference will begin to emerge – a rustic country or farm style, or alternatively a garden that is more neat and tidy, formal, bold or lush. Colours, plants

Above: Planning a mood board is often a clear indication where your garden style trends lie whether oriental or rustic or neat, trim and tidy.

chapter 3

Top: Colour is not simply flowers although they are the colour form we think of first in most cases.

Middle: The dramatic lime yellow foliage of Acer shirasawanum 'Aureum' *not only has beautiful form and texture but good colour too – especially for the colder regions of the country.*

Opposie page:

Top: Some plants such as these conifers and Yucca gloriosa 'Variegata' *have dramatic forms which require little or no attention to develop.*

Middle: Swathes of willowy textured Carex sp. *are ideal texture plants to add to more conventional plant selections.*

Bottom: Seasonal colour, both in summer and winter, such as these son-loving 'vincas' are an essential part of any garden.

and ornaments that you favour will feature in more and more of the material collected. Certain styles of hard landscape material will appeal more than others and you will begin to relate to the design of some garden structures more than others.

Visit homes with gardens that are architecturally similar to your own home; stroll through garden centres and nurseries and make lists of favourite pots, plants, garden featural elements such as statues, water features or garden furniture, and if necessary visit a paving company and tile supplier to see what could be underfoot. *Above all, ask questions.*

If your collected ideas depict more than one style that appeals to you, don't be discouraged or confused, some of them can be put to good use in smaller, more private areas of the garden, even if this happens at a later stage. If the garden has previously been designed and you enjoy some of its aspects, photograph these aspects and add them to the ever-expanding collection of thoughts and ideas.

There will come a time when the collection begins to repeat itself. Too much of the material collected is the same? This should be an indication of what you like and what not. At this stage it's likely that sufficient components for a mood board have been gathered.

Try not to make the board too big, too busy and too mixed when it comes to depicting a specific style of 'mood'. I find a board that is roughly A3 in size is generally large enough to display all the pieces gathered to suggest or clarify most images. How you combine them is up to you, after all the intention is to generate an atmosphere which you intend to convert into a garden style: pieces of tile, a few pebbles, small splashes of colour, bits of cloth, pictures and photographs are all grist to the mill – plus anything else you think may help to set the 'mood'.

Remember a mood board alone does not design the garden – it simply provides you with a range of inspirational materials, which if well combined (based on personal opinion of what has a 'feel good' aspect to it) will present you with a garden that appeals to you. Once you are satisfied that the mood board is a fair collection of images, colours and inspirations, it will probably help you think in a specific direction rather than have a head filled with a host of conflicting ideas.

To convert the board into a usable item gather all initial plans and observation notes together with the mood board in conjunction with the initial site plan, indicating where all the restraints, fixtures and influencing factors are.

You can begin to create a palette of ideas, starting with such aspects as paving ideas for the various areas, expanding to desirable garden components, such as patio thoughts, a specific pot, and so on, moving on to the favourite colours, plants, moods, atmospheres and preferred incidentals such as sculptures, garden lighting and furniture styles.

Remember I have warned against trying to find sets of rules to follow – they don't exist, but as previously mentioned there are guidelines that will make designing a personal space a little easier. Some of the guidelines that I wish to share with you are known as design principles. You will have noticed that while discussing the mood board I have made mention of colour and texture; these are part of an all-important aspect of garden design known as **design elements**.

There are four design elements, all of which need to be considered to pave the way to a better understanding of what makes a garden design successful.

Colour – helps to create 'mood' or atmosphere in the garden.

Form – can be regarded as the visual building blocks of the design, providing body and harmony.

Texture – strongly contributes to the style or collection of styles within the design.

Density – provides an element of solidity or airiness to the landscape.

Colour

Colour is as mysterious and as evanescent as the taste of water. So much has been written about colour from all points of view, rainbows, sunsets, the iridescence of oil on water, plants and manufactured colours of paints, dyes or cosmetics.

In solid colour there are three basic or primary colours (outlined in black in colourwheel below), which cannot be created by mixing any other colours together – red, blue and yellow. If these are mixed together in pairs we have secondary colours.

Blue and yellow make green and is complementary to red, red and yellow make orange, which is complementary to blue and blue and red make purple, complemented by yellow. The extent to which the two colours are combined will produce secondary colours favouring either the one colour of the other. If white is added to either primary or secondary

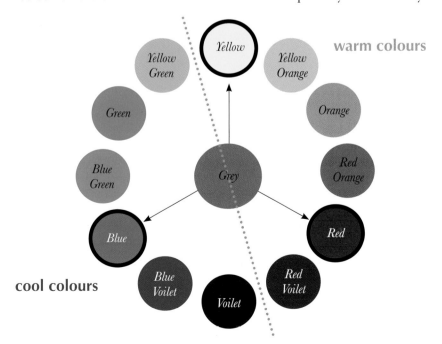

warm colours

Yellow

Yellow Green *Yellow Orange*

Green *Orange*

Blue Green *Grey* *Red Orange*

Blue *Red*

Blue Voilet *Voilet* *Red Voilet*

cool colours

Top: The vibrant plum and red foliage of Berberis thunbergii 'Rose Queen' *is a beautiful addition to any summer garden in almost all parts of South Africa where reasonable watering is possible, except perhaps the sub-tropical or coastal regions.*

Middle: Despite how roses look in winter there are not many gardeners that have not at some stage or another enjoyed their blooms, either on the plants or filling a bowl in the home.

Bottom: The blue-grey foliage of Aloe striata *makes this a worthwhile indigenous form plant even when not in flower.*

colours, the resultant pastel shades are referred to as tints and if black is added, the resultant deeper colours are referred to as tones.

The colour wheel, which moves through the colour spectrum of the rainbow starting with red, orange, yellow, on to green (the middle colour), then blue, indigo and finally violet is readily created in nature and it is this range of colours which interests the plant lover walking around a nursery, garden centre or home garden.

All too often when the word colour is mentioned in a design sense, there is a tendency to think only of flower colour, overlooking the fact that in many cases the flowers are an added seasonal bonus to the year-round effect of the plant. This means that despite the value of the flower colour and its effect at a specific time in the seasons, no garden can be created solely on floral colour and effect, without occasions when the garden would lack impact due to lack of flowers and hence colour.

Also there is often a tendency to overlook the fact that other than flowers there are numerous interpretations of colour: bark, berries, autumn and spring effects as well as the seasonal foliage of the plants. Foliage comes in a vast array of greens, not to mention a colour chart ranging from near-white, through pink, red, gold, purple, blue-grey, to deep black-green and in some cases near black, all without a flower in sight. What makes this aspect of colour so important is that in any garden design foliage has a far longer presence and more reliable impact than that based on flower colour alone.

However, this does not imply that flowers are not essential in the designing of a garden. Quite the opposite, in fact, because they play a major role in enhancing areas and aspects within the design framework. Imagine spring without flowering bulbs, annuals or early flowering trees and shrubs. And what role would these play in the lives of garden lovers if flowers were not essential? Remember, though, that the plants used in a design because of their flower colour should enhance the basic design when in flower rather than distract from it. If mistakes are made, the planting may only look attractive or balanced when certain plants come into flower and for the remainder of the seasons that area may appear rather drab.

Colour does not only relate to plants when considering a design, all the non-plant items must be considered as potential colour components. Hard landscape elements such as various forms of paving, stepping stones, pebbles, gravel, wood, rock as well as manufactured elements such as containers, furnishings and any painted surfaces will all combine with plants, to a greater or lesser degree, to help formulate the ideal design.

Much of the 'mood' in a design is created by incorporating the right colours and the right amount of colour within specific areas of the design. Colour is regarded as being warm – red, orange and yellow, or cool – green, blue and mauve (or purple and violet). White, grey, silver and black emphasise and add contrast to either the warm or cool colours. Depending on how these colours are used, a design can appear to be warm, bright, friendly – even uncomfortably hot if too much red is employed in too small a space – or cool if restful. In fact, cool colours tend to appear cold and uninviting in winter but are ideal in shaded areas in summer; the reverse applies when using the warm colours – think of the vibrant orange and yellow Namaqualand daisies flowering in mid-winter. An all-white garden, on the other hand, tends to appear as crisp and clinical, with little or no 'mood' at all.

The selective use of colour in a design has the capacity to visually change a site's dimensions. When warm colours are employed at the furthest extents of a long narrow garden space it tends to visually draw those areas nearer, while if cool colours are employed in a similar situation the depth of the site seems to taper off into a misty distance. Likewise, if warm colours are used in small areas close to places of regular activity such as pool or patio, there may be a feeling that the brightness in the limited space is oppressive and congested. However, if cool colours are utilised the space appears to open up and appear less overwhelming. As an alternative to using cool colours in small spaces, consider using pastel versions of the warm colours – lemon, apricot and pink rather than yellow, orange and red.

When selecting a range of colours to be employed in a design or sections of design, avoid the use of *all* colour options in one place, at the same time. This often results in 'over-kill' of the mood intended. Only in limited cases are 'riots' of colour effective – a tropical garden, an extensive rose garden or in 'natural' environments, yet even in these examples there is a balance of certain colours and an overall feeling of harmony. To quote Anna Pavord in her delightful book *Plant Partners – Creative Plant Combinations*: 'Most bedding schemes have too many colours in them. Three is plenty. Two is better.'

It is wise to avoid extreme colour *(see photo right)* contrasts in a design, such as yellow and purple or orange and blue. Although these combinations are often included in designs to create focus or depth in a design, the reverse is quite often the case: they jar and draw too much attention to unimportant or small areas within the design *(see photo below)*. 'Thinking only of colour can blind you to

the rest of the plant's attributes – or its faults' (Anna Pavord again in the same beautiful book). Rather select plants or items that have other redeeming features be- sides their colour, such as

Top: No cool shade area should be without the beautiful golden foliage of one of the many shade loving foliage plants such as this Aucuba japonica *variety to add light and colour.*

Middle: The colour of these containers will be a perfect compliment to the form plants and pebbles once planted.

Bottom: The vivid orange wall is a perfect background to the plants and hardware in this small townhouse garden. The mirror adds another dimensional element to the design too.

interesting textures or shapes. Although colour can be used in a focal sense, ideally it should be in harmony with the overall theme of that particular design – a harsh yellow tree or shrub will contribute little or nothing to a design where the overall mood or atmosphere is created by using muted greens and other cool colours.

Form

When considering and selecting plants for a design, size and shape are important visual aspects. All plants will attain a natural shape and final size if left to develop. The form or shape varies, but several standard forms have been identified. Natural form and size are not to be confused with those that are 'manufactured' by clipping the plants and by doing so controlling both their shape and size.

Plant shapes play an important role in developing a design, whether formal or informal in appearance. In most cases gardens tend to be more relaxed and informal in appearance, so the range of plant material available is reasonably extensive. However, there is a resurgence in formal designs, particularly where strong architectural themes are to be enhanced. It is important that the correct plant material is employed to create the desired form effects. In smaller garden spaces there is a need for 'tidy', naturally well-formed plants due to space limitations.

A word or two on plant sizes – try and clarify a plant's final height and width prior to incorporating it into a design. Many plants grow *much* larger in all directions than we are led to believe. Removal or constant pruning increases maintenance and reduces the effective lifespan of a garden if the wrong-sized plants are used. Similarly, if the plants don't grow big enough, it's often years of growth wasted before realisation sets in.

In almost all possible plant forms there are numerous size options – enquire first, and avoid mistakes later.

Typical **triangular forms** include *Cedrus deodara*, the ever-popular Christmas tree, and some other trees and conifer varieties. If the triangle is inverted there are numerous ornamental grasses, flowering fruit trees and New Zealand flax (*Phormium tenax*) varieties to choose from. Some plants

Like many other conifers these Cupressus macrocarpa 'Gold Crest' *have a tidy natural triangular shape making them ideal in situations where formality is called for.*

have an initial triangular form while young, which becomes more rounded as they mature.

Columnar form is also referred to as upright or fastigiated and is generally limited to some poplars (those famous Eastern Free State landmarks now best remembered in photographs and paintings, as they have largely been removed as a part of the invader plant control programme), 'church yard' cypress (*Cupressus sempervirens var. stricta*) and several other tall thin conifers and plant species. Perhaps a *Cordyline* or *Cussonia sp*, both known as Cabbage trees, could be incorporated in this form category, although rather for their height than their rounded crown. But in the annual and perennial plant choices there are beautiful delphiniums, hollyhocks and sunflowers to use for tall height.

Rounded form is well represented in an extensive range of plants from low growing annuals to large trees. Some of the forms hover between being round and triangular, and have a more oval appearance. This plant form is generally the most popular when selecting plants for an informal yet tidy planting. This is perhaps the most popular human-made form too, as numerous plants can be clipped into standard 'balls' or 'pom-poms'; even the over-the-top 'poodle-clipped' plants that are a series of rounded clipped balls on one plant!

The weeping form is often responsible for the softness and old-world charm of some older gardens, whether incorporated in the design as tree forms or cascading over walls and out of hanging baskets and containers. Sadly these plants are often pruned into 'oddities' that bear little or no resemblance to their natural shapes – weeping mulberry (*Morus alba pendula*), for example.

Flat-topped forms are common to many indigenous *Acacia* species in southern Africa, but few people realise that minus trunk or stem they become the ground-hugging, spreading form of many popular garden plants, more popularly known as groundcovers. Even a well-grown creeper rambling over a pergola can be considered a flat-topped plant.

Architectural plant forms are generally those that are not easily placed in other form groups. They generally have distinct shapes unique to that plant range, for example Aloes, tree ferns, bananas, palms, cycads, cacti and many other succulents as well as any other 'odd' plant species. These plants play a valuable creative and sculptural role in designs, often adding living stature or focal value when an inorganic item such as a statue would not be quite as effective or appropriate.

Informal or random form. Although there are many plants with reasonably tidy natural forms, there are others which when left to grow naturally are vigorous, untidy and inclined to take over areas larger than the gardener intended. Caution and space are necessary when selecting such plants: whether they become large or are limited in size, they require constant attention and maintenance when used in conjunction with more manageable plants. Bougainvillaea, Plumbago, rosemary, Cape honeysuckle (*Tecoma capensis*), Pride of De Kaap (*Bauhinia galpinii*) and

Top: Where space allows the large architecturally dramatic Agave sp *adds impressive form to what may otherwise have been a rather ordinary design.*

Centre: Many creepers such as this white form of the beautiful spring flowering Wisteria, Wisteria floribunda alba *can, if not kept under control, become large informal plants inter-twining among other plants growing nearby.*

Above: Several typical ground hugging ground covers will provide a pleasing alternative to lawn in some places in the design.

Opposite page:

Top: Consider all aspects of design when combining items especially if the intended design is small and reasonably focal. Here an antique pump, rocks and blue-grey Agave atenuata *combine perfectly at the base of a couple of palms near a pool-side.*

Middle: Careful selection of plant forms go a long way to creating the ideal atmosphere.

Bottom: Tidy rose standards planted above other plants provides a three dimensional effect in a limited space.

Top: Texture helps to set the mood intended such as the pleasing leafy contrasts under the trees.

Above: Some times the simpler the man-made form is the better. Here Murraya exotica *simply clipped in a spiral is dramatic in its final design form rather than its specific plant shaping*

Right: Clipped forms can create a spectacular focal point.

several creepers such as jasmine are typical examples of this vigorous plant form.

Clipped or man-made forms. Whenever there is a re-emergence of formality in landscape design, there is a need for ultra-formal plant forms. Plants clipped into cones, pyramids, balls, squared and whimsical forms such as birds, animals or abstract forms emerge from under the hand of the topiary artist. Generally these plants have small, compact, evergreen foliage that is able to withstand regular clipping. The plants are usually long-lived and the attention they require is intense and constant. Select these 'oddities' with care, knowing what is required to maintain them.

Form in a design will have bearing on all plants used in that design, however large or small, and combined with colour will begin to provide solidarity to the design, which up until now has been a mere collection of shapes on paper. As is the case with colour, consideration of form extends beyond the plants utilised to include the architecture of structures, hard landscape elements and aesthetic forms such as statuary, containers, and furniture and water features.

The attention given to form can be extended beyond the boundaries of a project to include surrounding areas and neighbouring organic and inorganic forms: even beyond, where applicable, to skylines, vistas and horizons. This is often referred to as 'borrowed landscapes'.

Texture

Texture is perhaps the most significant aspect of design, in as much as it appeals to both sight and touch. The roughness of some leaves or bark, the silkiness of others, the hard inflexibility or softness of some petals and the thorns, spines or barbs on many branches are all essential plant characteristics employed when combining plants in a design. The shadows they cast, their silhouettes, the way in which branches, leaves, fruit or flowers are arranged, are all elements relevant to the manner in which a plant can help in creating a specific style.

When creating a landscape or garden style for a particular area, the plants used will either enhance the atmosphere of the style intended or not. Bamboo, mossy foliage, autumn colours and compact small-leafed evergreen shrubs would imply an oriental style. To suggest a woodland atmosphere in parts of a garden, ferns, or fernlike foliage, lush evergreen, shade-tolerant perennials and moss could be effective, while palms, bold foliage and bright colours would suggest a tropical theme. In each of these instances the texture of the plant material used helps create the style or atmosphere intended.

Texture in a planting can be obtained by the successful combination of evergreen and deciduous material, whose seasonal changes can contribute to the changing 'feel' of the design. When these plant combinations are used in conjunction with the various hard landscape textures, such as pebbles alongside a groundcover, or gravel spread between stepping stones, and the textures obtained from shadows cast against walls, dappled shade on pathways or ponds are added, it becomes obvious that visual or tactile textures offer endless opportunities in the garden.

The need to touch and the instinctive need to smell plants often bring another aspect to the texture range of design contributions – that of sensory designs often used for handicapped persons, where the textures encourage them to make contact with the plants, learning to identify elements of the design by their 'feel' and often their scent too.

As with the previous two elements, texture has important applications when considering how to combine hard landscape elements. Consider the rough or smooth texture of walls and floor coverings, such as gravel, its size, the smoothness of pebbles, the rough or sanded surface of wood.

Top: Simply by selecting the right plant types the atmosphere is set without too much in the way of accessories – such as this soft fern and 'moss-like' planting at the base of a palm near a brick pathway.

Above: The combining of HLE textures with plants often enhances both aspects to form a more whole atmosphere in the design.

Far left: The hard texture of newly emerging Cycad foliage gives a feeling of solidness despite the newness of the foliage.

Left: HLE such as pebbles will also help in creating the right 'feel' of a part of a design where plants alone may prove to be too unassuming.

Top: Large foliage on long stems does not always imply a high level of density as this Philodendron selloum *implies.*

Centre: A balanced planting scheme will generally offer the best form of density in a conventional garden setting.

Bottom: Coleonema album – *white confetti bush, is denser than larger more loose foliaged plants.*

Not only will this add visual considerations to the design, it will create contrast or harmony within the design at the same time.

Density

This is the one remaining element in a fully three-dimensional garden design. Strangely, it is the element most often overlooked. Simply put, density in a garden implies that consideration is given to where dense, 'can't see through' type plants are needed and where more 'transparent', sparsely foliaged plants can be used. The reason for this is not only to create enclosed, private areas, as one may need at a patio or swimming pool, but to avoid seeing the whole landscape at one time and creating areas of interest to be visited and perhaps surprised by. Often, when a garden has a closed, oppressive or crowded feeling it is because too many dense-foliaged plants have been used.

The level of density of a plant is largely attributable to the size and amount of foliage and how it is arranged on the plant, under normal growing conditions. For example, the large, impressive foliage of a tree fern *Cyathea sp* or *Philodendron selloum* is sparsely arranged on long stems, resulting in large open spaces between the foliage – this would not offer satisfactory screening potential. In contrast to this, the fine, very small foliage of most conifers, confetti bush (*Coleonema pulchellum*) or some Melaleuca species is so closely arranged on the plant, and so prolifically, that seeing beyond this type of plant is almost impossible.

When reference is made to a design that has been designed to create 'rooms within rooms', density is an aspect which must be given serious consideration so that each area remains distinct – in this way more than one 'mood' or style can be created within one single space, without one style conflicting with any others. In many historic gardens this sense of various 'garden rooms' was achieved by using 'wall-like' plantings of tall dense hedges, but a preference for low maintenance has reduced this option to a range of unclipped, dense-foliaged plants.

Density needs to be considered as important when creating other aspects of a design and when selecting plants for a hedge or windbreak. When selecting plants that will provide dappled shade over a pathway or semi-shade tolerant plants the density or lack of it would play a major role. In instances where there is a need to see through a design to a specific area, viewpoint or focal aspect the plants chosen need to be more transparent in or through any intervening plant areas than in the surrounding areas so that there will be continual glimpses of the area or item of attraction.

Seasonal density is also important, particularly when considering the functional aspects of design. Deciduous trees planted for parking area shade are often more functional if the shade is less dense in winter, when all the leaves have fallen; similarly trees planted to provide summer shade to bedrooms or patio areas are more functional if sunlight can penetrate through them during the colder winter months. On the other hand, the wrong choice of plant type can result in sparseness when it is least desired, near swimming pools, patios or boundaries.

Although erecting structures or building walls can create a sense of density, the desired tendency is rather to use plant material to create internal screening. There are some situations though where an element of screening is needed quicker than plants can provide. In such situations, free-standing lattice panels or trellis can be utilised, either unadorned or in conjunction with quick-growing or seasonal creepers such as sweet peas, runner beans or black-eyed Susan (*Thunbergia alata*).

Awareness of these four design elements makes it easier to select the plants (and hard landscape elements) that will make for a successfully designed garden. The satisfaction of designing surroundings that you are comfortable with becomes more attainable with each step. None of these steps are complicated and the more of them we cover, the easier designing becomes.

Above: Glimpses of garden 'rooms' beyond a well planted screen creates interest in any garden.

Top right: Sometimes a progressive series of hedges – if space allows – not only provides required privacy, but visual interest too.

Centre right: In areas with limited space, a creeper grown against a sturdy screen will, as it develops, provide all the density required, but may demand regular pruning to stay in place.

Above: A simple, reasonably low planting combining colour, form as well as texture can often provide ideal privacy in areas that are elevated. Particularly where there are neighbours on a similar visual level.

SCALE AND OTHER DESIGN PRINCIPLES

Now that design elements are firmly tucked under your belt – they made a whole lot of sense too, didn't they? – I want to move on to design principles. These are simple descriptions of basic landscape design terminology. Perhaps up until now you haven't given them a whole lot of thought, but generally they are common sense and quite obvious once explained.

Scale

The principle with the most impact on designing any space is *scale*. I know that aspects of scale have been dealt with, but as mentioned, it can be interpreted in several ways. The visual relationship between plants and other plants, as well as hard landscape components, buildings or other structures and the people who have to live with them, is an important aspect of scale. Scale in this sense can be regarded as a visual relationship between various elements in a design. When any object or aspect is introduced into a design and causes all other aspects of the design to appear too large or unacceptably small, this object or aspect is said to be out of scale with the rest of the design. The ideal relationship is where no part of the design distorts any part or all of a design; it is then said to be *in scale.*

Above: Thin Aloe barberi *stems emphasise the thin elegance of the architecture.*

Largely scale is relevant to people and 'human scale' is that sense of being comfortable when interacting with a design. Any design where the user feels crowded, overwhelmed or lost, as happens when standing alone in tall, dense, overgrown scrubby growth or on a vast open space where you are the biggest item around; such as a large playing field or a huge field of wheat, for example, is a design that will be underutilised and generally unpopular from a 'user friendly' point of view. This goes part way to emphasising the need for plants and other garden elements to be relatively well proportioned with regards to people. Garden design must enhance the scaled link between the property, the house, and the users. A large double-storey home is made to appear part of a property by incorporating trees of various sizes into the design; similarly shrubberies that incorporate lower growing plants towards the 'front' (or the area they are generally seen from) encourage attention and a visual relationship develops between the users and the design.

There are times when an exaggerated scale is called for, the Eiffel Tower and the American Statue of Liberty, for example. This is a form of shock scale design intended to create a dramatic reaction. The concept can be reversed to appeal to the size of young users, where all aspects of the design would appear to have a functional yet visually diminished scale, as is the case in children's gardens, miniature golf courses, petting zoos and some theme park areas. Both of these extremes can be employed to some extent in the domestic garden context. For example, a larger-than-life entrance area with imposing gates and large containers and tall mature palm trees, or alternatively an area allocated to a small play house with play equipment, kiddie-sized furniture and flower beds filled with plants that don't grow too large – both in their own way have a dramatic impact on the users.

Above: Tall plant material, in this case palms, add dramatic scale to the limited garden space.

Top and left: The dramatic scale of the sculpture is enhanced by the vista it oversees while the large 'flower pot man' would enthral any young child.

The scale of an open garden space is harder to relate to than the scale of rooms with furniture and fittings, and this is partially why landscape designs that have been developed with a 'rooms within a room' concept in mind tend to be more popular than the large, simple, open designs. The balanced smaller spaces with a ceiling, walls, a floor of living material, and related components, enhance the feeling of a 'human scale' relationship.

Link this to what I said about size and form of plants – you see it begins to make sense!

How do we accurately set out the various areas of the design to the

Above left: The correct choice of plant material is important in small areas to create the ideal 'human' related scale in these areas.

Above right: Even a canopy of mature trees will enhance the scale of a simple design.

Top left: Simple easy curves give a design an uncluttered appearance − simplicity often being the key word.

Top right: Some of the design principles discussed are simply good common sense to some experienced garden makers, such as keeping beds simple.

Centre: Dramatic foliage contrasts often add ideal balance in situations where much of the foliage texture is too similar.

Bottom: Balance is also dependant on the visual combination of plant choices.

desired size, particularly if these dimensions are specific 'mathematical' shapes? As the design progresses, land forms or shapes of certain areas will emerge as part of the design. These shapes are generally adjacent to or among fixed structures such as walls, corners, edges of things such as paving and pools or single standing items such as taps or trees. Use the positions of these fixed structures to help determine the positions of newly added design elements.

Simple curves are easy to reproduce:

On the plan, measure the narrowest and widest sections of the curve in relation to a fixed item such as a boundary or house wall. Insert stakes or markers at the narrowest and widest points of the curve and link them together with a sun-warmed hosepipe. Knock in stakes or markers along the curve at one or two metre intervals, remove the hosepipe (I have seen many a good hosepipe stabbed to pieces), and mark with a spade, pick or chalk dust.

It is just as simple to incorporate circles in a design. Fix the position of the circle's centre relevant to other areas within the design, by triangulation (see Chapter 2 for information on this process). Knock in a stake or peg at this point, making sure that if soil has to be removed or added, the stake/peg is deep enough into the soil and tall enough above it to remain there after the soil level has been changed. Tie a length of string loosely to the stage/peg and knot a loop into the string at the length of the radius of the circle. Through this loop insert a wooden or metal peg and tighten (re-measure the radius if in doubt *before* drawing the circle!) Once the circle has been drawn, leave the string in place to confirm construction phases or knock thin stakes along the drawn circle edge no further apart than 50-60 cm. These can be joined with string if necessary.

Setting out a triangle is a little trickier. Measure all three sides and their distance to other fixed components, such as corners, trees or taps. Measure two of the corners of the triangle to the same two fixed points. From one of the fixed points, using a peg inserted at the fixed point and a string with a marker attached (as for drawing the circle), draw part circles equal to the distance of the two corners of the triangle from the fixed point. These measurements will cross those drawn first; where they cross are the two corners of the triangle. Insert pegs at these two positions. Attach string to these two pegs and using the distances between each of these corners and the third corner, draw part circles. Where they cross is the position of the third corner of the triangle.

Similarly, by measuring to a fourth point an oblong or square can be accurately drawn. More tricky shapes may need the assistance of surveyors, builders or similar experienced help. Take time to measure accurately, if the final design relies on these shapes and their positions.

Although scale as a design principle is important when creating a user-friendly landscape, it is by no means the only one. There are a few others, all of which deal with the position of things, how many to use, how often, and so on. Most keen gardeners have been subconsciously applying these design principles for years. There is no great mystery about it, but awareness of them does help to make life a little easier if you're starting out new and inexperienced.

These principles are important to the creating of any design and they help create a design with a specific message rather than simply being a jumble of plants and structures. A successful design will have incorporated the design principles, irrespective of size of terrain, position or amount of fixed structures on the site or the particular needs of the user.

Other design principles

Balance – 'all things feeling equal'

There are two distinct approaches to the use of balance in a landscape design – formal or symmetrical balance, and informal or asymmetrical balance. How they are utilised will determine the final appearance of the design.

Symmetrical balance will create formality in the areas that it is applied to. Plants and accessories are planted or placed in even numbers in symmetrical positions on either side of an imaginary central line – the axis. The one side of the design is an exact mirror image of the other side. Depending on the architectural style of the structures, this is an ideal way of strongly emphasising an entrance area and visually or physically directing people to other important aspects of the home, or to emphasise visual direction to a focal point.

In instances where the formal design combines both structural and plant material, the tendency is to culminate the design at a definite point such as a fountain, summer house, formal rose or herb garden, reflecting pool or piece of appropriate sculpture. Despite the regular re-emergence of classical architectural styles, the formal garden can have its limitations, due to the reasonably high level of upkeep and the limited plant and accessory range, resulting in constant repetition for effect. This last aspect begins to limit individuality and opportunities to create a personalised garden.

The informal or asymmetrical use of balance, on the other hand, provides numerous opportunities for individuality. Here the visual 'weight' of a plant or other design component is balanced against other plants or components in a design, either by considering their density, size, quantity or intensity of colour or texture. What this means is that the plants are grouped together in such a way that no individual plant overwhelms its neighbours. For example, small, soft, fine-textured plants would have to be used in quantity if they were to be visually in balance with the large tree under which they were growing. Similarly, medium-sized trees and shrubs with light-coloured foliage and bright flowers would be planted on a property to balance the impact of a standard sized, single story, dark brick home. Too many dark-foliaged plants would enhance the dark structure and this could lead to a sombre visual

Top and centre: An invisible 'line' evenly divides a symmetrical or formal design generally with one central focal element

Above: Formality creates a feeling of simple classic elegance when used on a large scale.

Top: Repeated use of dramatic plant forms - such as Encephalartos sp's are an ideal way of creating rhythm.

Centre: Variety in a design is best created by grouping various plants, with similar growing conditions, together in a balanced planting scheme.

Above: Repeated use of HLE along with plant material gives a strong design message.

Right: By repeating a HLE design in the landscape the eye is led to areas of importance, such as the front door.

impact (refer to 'Styles' – Chapter 8). They need to be combined with, for example, smaller and more numerous plants to provide an informal yet visually balanced combination. Generally uneven quantities – 1, 3, 5, or 7 – are used (three smaller, darker trees or shrubs may offset and thus balance one large, lighter foliaged tree, for example).

Rhythm – swing-time – 'garden style'

This principle can also be described as 'flow' or 'line' in a design and is used to prevent monotony and create a sense of design movement and provide continuity to the design. In other words it holds the various aspects of a design together visually. Brick mowing edges are an ideal way of creating rhythm.

Rhythm is linked to repetition, and the manner in which any component is repeated will influence the rhythm of the design. Repeating plants that are all similar in size, distance apart or appearance creates *static rhythm*. Repeating selected plants or hard landscape elements achieves *continuous rhythm* in sequence; alternatively, a single element, which varies in size and distance apart, can be used for the same effect. *Progressive rhythm* is created by using elements that do not stay the same size and either increase or decrease in size as they are used through the design.

Variety – 'adding floral spice to life'

When there is too much repetition (too much of too few varieties) in a design it can tend to be boring or monotonous. Variety will brighten a design and at the same time add interest. Adding the elements of design – colour, form, texture and density – will automatically incorporate variety.

Combining plants and hard landscape element that create various contrasts within the design will generally create variety. Fine-foliaged plants alongside ones with larger, coarser foliage are a simple yet endless combination opportunity to ensure appealing variety. But be careful! The over-extended use of variety will result in a 'botanical zoo' look rather than a design.

Repetition – 'a rose is a rose is a rose!'

This concept can hold a design together by the repeated use of an item, a container, plant or colour. A simple example of this would be the repeat planting of street trees that give a street a feeling of unity despite the various buildings behind them in the street. Repetition tends to lead the eye from near aspects of a design to those that are furthest away. It is an ideal way to shorten the visual length of a panhandle driveway or to subconsciously shorten the length of a long, narrow property.

Succession – 'visual leapfrog'

Succession is the articulation of spaces or shapes in a design which results in progression and development of the design. In other words, by using structures or dramatic sculptural plants the viewer is subconsciously led to areas of major importance or from one important area to another.

This could be enhanced by the use of dramatic containers at points of interest. Another way in which progression can be obtained is by incorporating patterns in simple components such as paving: this is a typical technique employed in the walkways of shopping malls and open plazas.

Simplicity – 'less is more'

This does not imply a boring design, rather an imaginatively simple use of plants and hard landscape elements, chosen for their specific contribution. These limited elements, when combined, are able to develop fully into a specific yet simple design such as well-placed street furniture of a specific style that flows through a design.

Massed rather than random plantings attain simplicity by creating larger areas of the same element rather than competing individuals. Repetition of plant species, construction elements, colours, forms, textures or design styles are several of the ways of creating simplicity.

Unity – 'garden design togetherness'

Unity in the landscape is defined as the balance or coherence of its components, yet at the same time allowing opportunities for variations in that design. Remember that a garden design is not static – there may be an occasion for change!

The most effective way to create coherent unity in a design is to be aware of the plant elements such as colour, form, texture and density.

Line – of a physical nature

There is always an exception that proves the rule: in a garden or landscape design this exception is *line*. It's not really an oddity, but used more often than not in a very strange manner: all squiggly and labour intensive – almost as if the more bends, swerves, bulges or hollows the line has the better or more effectively it has been employed. Whether the line is real or imaginary, it is wise to keep it simple so that it readily adheres to all the above-mentioned principles. After all, it's often simply a line between two aspects of the design – lawn and shrubbery, hard surface and lawn or planted areas, and so on. It is not intended to distract from or compete with the more important aspects of the design or appear as a major component of the design. Should the 'line' principle be used as an item of impact, such as a pattern in paving, walls, planting schemes and so on, then it would need to be treated as a specific design item.

When line is shown in a design there is often confusion as to what exactly is being referred to. I don't mean the way the eye flows or doesn't flow through a design (more easily interpreted as rhythm or flow), but rather the physical use of lines – bed edges, shape of paths or alternative surfaced areas and any other ways in which a line can be used to help create a design. Of course, design lines should complement the visual movement in the design so that indirectly the physical line remains a tangible example of a design principle.

Top: Maintenance of mass plantings can be easier than caring for a variety of plants in one area.

Centre: A mix of succulents collectively grown for their colour.

Above: The effective yet time-consuming use of ivy as a dramatic art form.

A simple yet eye-catching effect of this 'floral' furniture.

Top row left: A grouping of impressive containers dramatically used, is certain to be an eye-catching element in any design.

Top row centre: By making the feature nestle into the plants it adds atmosphere without being overwhelming.

Top row right: Any decorative item added to a garden should enhance the design rather than detract from it.

Bottom row left: The WOW-factor of an extremely unusual water feature.

Bottom row centre: This dramatic metal swirled sculptural is sure to catch any visitor's attention.

Bottom row right: Some times the uniqueness of the item requires a specific setting so as not to overwhelm the design.

Emphasis – 'wow!'

Depending on what literature is referred to, this rather overrated and oft-misunderstood aspect of design is alternatively known as a focal point, accent, feature, or area of attention. The idea is that the various areas within a design should have some aspect of interest, so that the eye is led *to* an area in the design rather than vaguely *through* it.

Avoid creating more than one focal point in any one part of the garden. This will cause conflict and clutter the design. A simple rule of thumb is that if one area of emphasis is seen, any others should be behind the viewer or in other parts of the garden, out of sight. I wish to warn against an over-awareness of 'fashion' of focal points which could lead to garden design being crowded with pointless gimmicks used as focal points. These 'focal points' tend to conflict with the intended design and distract from it and its sustainability as a well-designed space. It is equally important to incorporate focal elements that will enhance the proposed style of design – no garden gnomes in an oriental-styled design, please!

Needless to say, if the desired or perfect element is not instantly – or even for various seasons – available, don't let that stop you! Perfect your design in such a way that it still has appeal and charm despite the missing 'final' element. When the item has been acquired and added to the garden the overall effect should automatically be enhanced further by it being there.

Because such a vast range of materials can be employed to create focal elements – from mass-produced containers, water features, garden lights and other accessories to the more imaginative and often specifically created items such as hand-crafted containers, purpose-built furniture or water features and ponds – it is possible to want a 'little bit of everything'. Take your time finding the right item, it's far more gratifying in the long run!

Don't forget that 'less is more', even with 'wow' effects! If a fountain is too tall, a water feature too complicated and vast, if containers in a limited space are too bright or too big, or a design in a paved area is so dominant as to be overwhelming, then the intended effect of any focal element is lost. It becomes something that distracts, jars or is out of keeping and proportion with all of its surroundings.

A ROOM WITH A VIEW

All forms of home-related design inevitably have a lot to do with rooms ... rooms in many forms, with many uses. A garden is simply an outdoor extension of a home, so it's expected that the outdoor space will, somehow or another, be compartmentalised into what could be perceived to be garden or outdoor rooms.

The simplest form of this is one uncluttered, large room covering the entire property, with an expanse of lawn extending almost from one end of it to the other and used for everything: the dog, car repairs, family events, kiddies' play areas as well as a quiet corner – and it may even have some form of a vegetable patch or compost heap relegated to one of the corners.

Suffice it to say that this is hardly a designed room or space. It is simply an 'open' piece of land surrounding a structure and quite unable to add any atmosphere to the property, let alone provide shelter, privacy or interesting aspects to look at from inside the home or any other part of the garden. For some, this is an ideal garden, simple to maintain – but then these are not the home owners who are intent on owning a designed space surrounding their home, in fact, generally they are contented landowners rather than 'gardeners' in the dedicated sense of the word.

For those with their hearts set on conjuring a designed garden from a blank space, it is important that this space is seen as it is from various angles. Perhaps an ideal position to start from would be to look at it from various positions inside the home, particularly from rooms that are used to relax in. This makes the bathroom facilities a low priority, while the lounge, patio, family room and major bedrooms could be more important than study, guest bedrooms or dining room.

Above: An eye-catching water 'rill' seen from indoors brings sound and movement 'into' the home.

chapter 5

Whatever the levels of importance, I suggest that the view into the outdoor space is carefully considered from each room. This is not a case of simply looking to the boundaries of the property, but beyond them too. In some cases a superb view is experienced from a single room and nowhere else in the home. Similarly, an unsightly view can be experienced when looking out from rooms that are in constant use.

It is equally important to view the entire garden from important areas *outside* the house, such as the approach from the street or the view of proposed utility areas from areas with a more recreational function.

Now is a good time to consider how dominant the structures are; things like size of windows, and how many windows and openings there are in one area of the home. How close are the structures to the boundaries, and will there be sufficient space to garden between the two? Is privacy a factor? If there are balconies on upper levels, look into the outdoor spaces from these levels, as there is a decidedly different feeling of space, and the views seen from these elevated areas are often quite different.

A lack of space outside the rooms when looking outwards from the structure needs to be taken into consideration. Earlier I mentioned that realistic scale must be carefully considered – how in-scale are the structures in relation to the land space available? This is of key importance in the cluster or townhouse development where space (and privacy), are often critical and a garden appears to be squeezed between structures. Considering this aspect of scale will perhaps call for clever screening or selective plant use to help link various large or closely situated structures.

Above: Detailed planting of a narrow area helps detract from the nearness of neighbours.

Above: Make sure that the addition of outdoor rooms such as a gazebo are well positioned or they tend to become unused 'oddities'.

Below: The 'quiet and secluded' design treatment is an ideal way to add character to odd parts of the garden.

The purpose of this simple exercise is to determine what will need to be incorporated into the design to ensure fullest use of the property in a realistic as well as visually pleasing way. It begins to suggest where to screen, plant large trees or shrubs, build walls or position personal family areas such as swimming pools, gazebos, lapas, garden cottages or summer houses. It is an ideal way of deciding where the most secluded quiet areas are, and for designing that 'get away from it all' area in the garden. Incidentally, it will also provide positions for outdoor service areas such as refuse, compost, storage or general utility areas where, for example, extra parking can be provided.

The more specific the needs of the family or user of the entire outdoor space, the more important this small exercise in observation will be.

A well designed pool or water feature will add great visual value to any garden.

Above: Scale is important when introducing any element, such as this rock column water feature, to a limited space.

Relating the outdoor areas to indoor spaces should help clarify how the outdoor space is to be divided between 'rooms' of unrelated activities. In most gardens these 'rooms' are created subconsciously, largely relevant to the rooms of the home. So service areas lead off from kitchen and laundry areas or driveway and service entrances while the patio and living rooms will extend into recreational 'rooms' such as pool, lapa or extended multifunctional outdoor paved areas. However, often because of lack of space to physically divide the areas by means of plants or structures or a combination of both, or simply because of the lack of inclination, there are situations where spaces overlap, services clash with recreational activities, spaces are too confined for the intended uses and generally the feeling is that the 'outdoor rooms' don't quite solve the problem. Too many ideas incorporated into one garden design can often be more of a headache than a totally non-designed open space.

Let's take a closer look at the possible requirements of some outdoor areas.

The pool/fishpond area

- Try to keep these areas in **sunny positions**. Constant shade over swimming pools or ponds leads to all sorts of maintenance problems.

- Position them **near recreational areas** of the home such as a patio, family room or where they can be seen from the living quarters of the home. This is not only for their visual effect as part of the garden design but also for reasons of safety and maintenance. There is less likelihood of swimming pool or fishpond mishaps if they are in full sight of other areas of activity and the need to keep them clean in such a position is obvious.

- Decide on the position and size of the **surrounding space** required for extended activities. Do this before the area is enclosed or the pond or pool is built. All too often the area is too small and as a result is not utilised to its fullest extent, since related activities occur elsewhere.

- Keep the size of these structures practical, **in scale with the area** available and where possible in keeping with the style of the house. (Obviously if these structures exist at the time of redesigning or designing the garden the best has to be made of what is at hand.)

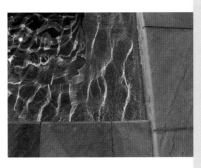

- If the **area surrounding the pool** is limited, consider using paving of one sort of another rather than plants or lawn. Consider planting in raised planters or using a selection of portable containers.

- **Avoid the temptation to plant trees** (including palms) any nearer than 3 metres from the edge of any water-containing structure, however large or small. Root pressure may cause leaks that are generally costly to repair – and heaven forbid that a well-grown plant may have to be removed at a later stage!

- It is wise to look around to see **what trees are growing in the neighbouring gardens** before positioning a pool or pond, as their long-term impact on these structures is beyond your control and could intensify maintenance considerably. (Needless to say your trees will have a similar impact on a neighbour's property: it makes for stress-free good neighbourliness to avoid these situations where possible.)

- Take care to **use non-skid surfaces** surrounding swimming pool areas and steer clear of spiky plant material. Pay particular attention to the choice of surfaces if salt chlorinators are used to keep the water clean, as salt has a destructive impact on some surfaces (including the quality of the soil) – perhaps consider natural stone products.

- Where possible try to **conceal the filtration system** in such a way that it is accessible but does not have an adverse impact on the general design of the area.

Above left: The correct treatment of a pool edge will ensure that the pool or pond is in harmony with its surroundings.

Above: In the case of a large focal element, such as this simple rectangular pool, make sure that there is space to move around it.

Bottom: An outdoor shower area with a difference and easy to maintain too.

The private area

- This **need not be too large** an area and is often an ideal way of utilising an odd out-of-the way area large enough to include a bench, small table and chairs, a hammock slung between trees or a frame under trees. It is often ideally suited to areas on the **south side of homes** where it is reasonably cool and shady.

- There **is little need for lawn**; this is an ideal place to incorporate rustic paving, groundcovers and some small form of water feature, sculpture or garden lighting.

- Because these are generally smaller areas, try to **scale down the elements** to be used, such as the size of paving material, water features, and so on. If containers are wanted, then consider using more small ones.

- As these areas are generally incompatible with the busy, noisy, family entertainment areas it would be an idea if these areas are **kept well away from other areas of activity.**

Left: Small detailed water features are all that some areas need for impact.

Centre: If space is limited, screening walls may be necessary to separate the various parts of the garden

Right: Attention to the small details adds extra character.

Dramatic accessories generally require perfect positioning to have the right impact.

- As they are not generally used on an ongoing basis by large groups of people they can happily be **combined with bird-feeding or bird-watching** activities where the birds are not constantly disturbed and finally move to other areas – outside your garden.

The family area

- Often designed to **extend the living area** from inside the house, via the patio, into the garden – thus increasing the general living and recreational area.

- This is the one area of design where there is often a need for **added construction** such as a gazebo, summer house (maybe a lapa!), permanent braai facilities or the like to enhance outdoor living. It is a good idea to design these structures as part of the overall design, but to build them before any general landscaping and planting takes place.

- It is important that **realistic scale** is considered when planning such an area, to ensure that sufficient space is provided for both the users and their equipment or furniture.

- Although these areas tend to consist largely of various hard landscape and building materials, don't overlook the opportunity to incorporate built planters or leave open spaces in the paving to allow for the **softening effect of plants** as part of the design. The planters allow for really dramatic plant use to add that special atmosphere – cycads, palms, aloes and tree ferns come to mind.

- I suggest that these often rowdy and active areas should be **screened from the more restful areas** of the home, such as bedrooms.

This helps to reduce family conflict and guarantees a good Sunday afternoon nap.

Entrance, driveway and parking

Despite being the area of **first impression**, this entire area is often left to its own devices. However, it is essential for the smooth running of a home, simply because this is the way in and out and for parking of vehicles in-between.

- Make sure that the area allocated is **large enough** to accommodate existing vehicles as well as those that may visit – and those that are added to the 'family fleet' with time as kids grow up and older relations move in.

- Remember that vehicles need specific areas and distances to reverse or turn – and that reducing these areas makes life difficult ... for ever!

- Keep **shade** trees in these areas at least 2 metres from the edge of any hard surfaces to prevent damage caused by roots.

- In **limited spaces** consider shaded carports rather than trees which may cause damage to paving as they grow large enough to cast sufficient shade.

- Make this area **inviting**, remembering that it is the area of initial impact for guests. It should be interesting yet practical, with decent width of pathways, a clear indication as to which direction people should move in and where the entrance to the home is.

- This is an ideal opportunity for the introduction of a **focal point** – a water feature, sculpture or other form of garden art, colourful plantings that change interestingly with the seasons – annuals, effective perennials or dramatic flowering shrubs or specimen plant forms adding drama to the style of the house.

- Remember that this area is generally the only **access and outlet for services**. Delivery of heater oil, gas or coal will arrive through this entrance area, as well as the removal of refuse, garden rubble ... including the furniture if a major move is made. Steer clear of fancy low covered arch type entrances if larger than normal vehicles are expected to drive in and out.

- Provide ample safe parking for a **few extra vehicles** if space allows. This need not apply to complex developments, as visitors' parking is often provided for as part of the overall complex layout.

- Despite the fact that this is a first impression area, the material used should be **practical and durable**. Pay particular attention to the surfaces. Make sure that the product used will be sustainable. It should not weather, like some bricks or slasto, or erode as loose gravel or sand surfaces can, or begin to break up if not used often enough, like a tarred surface.

Top: Try to make any entrance garden inviting and interesting.

Bottom: The entrance area is an ideal place to add elements of special or unique interest, such as this 'family' of children sculptures.

Top: Even small spaces at the front door allow for an individual 'stamp' of the home owner.

Centre and below: The service areas need to be seen as parts of the overall garden design especially if space is limited. It can often be an ideal place to grow something interesting in a container.

Service areas

- Areas set aside for wash lines or other forms of clothes drying should have some hard surface to prevent dropped clothes from getting dirty.

- Make sure the areas for clothes hanging are large enough to manoeuvre in – often with a wash-basket in hand.

- If the service area is to be used as a short-term holding area for pets make sure that there is enough space for the pets to exercise, that there is a form of shade – either from trees or a structure, that there is a fresh water source and the surface can be kept hygienically clean – the inclusion of a tap in this area is always a good idea.

- If the area is to be used for outdoor storage of such items as boats, trailers or caravans, measure the item and make sure that sufficient space is provided to get the item in, parked and out again without major manoeuvring.

- Refuse areas as well as areas allocated to garden refuse or compost making are best floored with a hard surface to prevent slow hollowing out of the area with time and for washing or sweeping clean when required.

- If the area is enclosed make sure the gate(s) are large enough to remove the refuse easily – consider the width of a wheelbarrow to start with.

- Although the service areas are best concealed from other parts of the garden, they need to be accessible without having to impact on surrounding areas.

- Where possible, try to combine several service requirements into one area and provide a common access and exit point for storage or removal of items.

- Although service areas are often regarded as non-garden areas there is no reason that the 'green' aspect of these areas should be ignored. They prove to be ideal areas to plant trees and screening plants as alternative options to solid walls and gates and are an ideal area to grow herbs or vegetables in containers.

- Although a fruit or vegetable area is not strictly regarded as a service – and can be incorporated into any part of a design, they are often coupled to other service requirements for practical purposes, so that compost making, garden refuse disposal, a garden shed, an outdoor working surface (for machine maintenance) and fruit or veg growing can be housed in one compact practical area. If this is the case, remember to incorporate a tap and if possible an outdoor electrical point too.

Needless to say, these are simply guidelines: the needs of each individual and the available space to work with will have a major impact on the use of these suggestions in a design. Despite this, each one of these suggestions will help make designing of any garden space that much easier simply by helping to categorise thinking before planning.

WALLS, FLOORS AND CEILINGS

Having explored the possibility of creating 'rooms' for various applications, the next logical step is to determine what materials can be used to design these rooms. As a rule, at this stage of designing there is a reasonably comprehensive and accurate site plan available. The next step in the process is to create a *zone* or *bubble diagram* (plan), which will help to decide which 'rooms' will go where.

The zone or bubble diagram is a simple means of roughly indicating all the specific activities intended by the home owner as well as all other relevant information gathered relating to the site. The functions of the various parts of the garden are drawn as simple bubbles or zones. It is easy to plan communication routes (pathways, gates to closed-off areas, large service areas such as outside the kitchen or driveway and major activity areas). The bits left over are usually where the beds are created and filled with plant material.

These zone or bubble sketches *(see example on page 112)* indicate the intended size of the various areas of activity as well as how they relate to the entire property and one another. It is easy to see at this stage if an area allocated is too large or hopelessly too small; at the same time the sketches give an indication of how much space is available for plant material.

From these rough sketches it will also be possible to see where narrow areas will need to be divided by means other than plants – such as walls or wood panels – and where large, interesting plantings will be possible. Generally these large planting areas are where trees can be incorporated without them killing off lawn at a later stage or lifting paving as their root systems mature.

As the various areas are drawn on the plan (print several copies of the site plan to draw all these rough sketches on), name them and include all relevant notes specific to the area. 'Need wind barriers here', 'must level this area more', 'shallow rock outcrop here – move pond idea to here', and so on. The reason for this is that small specific details may otherwise be overlooked in the bigger picture,

leading to lost time as problems necessitate rethinking or redesigning a particular area.

Although creating these bubbles or zones is a simple process and serves as a general reminder of *what* is to happen and *where*, this process gives no indication as to *how* the effects are to be designed and what physical materials will be used. So as the 'rooms' are considered, a closer look at possible materials is necessary.

When planning a bubble or zone diagram, try to create a flowing movement through the various areas. This simple, comfortable movement not only indicates the path of communication from one area to another (in-house areas included), but also prevents those frustrating eventualities such as dragging the hose pipe or wheelbarrow across the patio, by indicating the most practical maintenance routes.

Above: Keep the surfaces simple and easy to maintain as well as in keeping with the overall design.

Durable surfaces need not be uninteresting as long as they are practical.

The floor

Although all plant material plays an important role in surface covering (given that most plants cover floor space anyway), I cover these extensively in the next chapter and choose to keep my floor, wall and ceiling thoughts to alternative options rather than plants.

Obviously most outdoor activities take place at ground level and depending on the specific activity, there is a huge range of materials from which to choose ideal surface coverings. The choice of these materials will go hand in hand with the designed style of this particular garden space (this will apply as the function of each outdoor 'room' is designed). Obviously the flooring/surface covering chosen should accentuate, enhance or offset the general architecture and other construction materials used within that same area.

At this stage an all-important aspect of garden design should make itself felt – that of sustainability, in other words, the design's realistic ability to survive, be durable, practical, aesthetic and functional, all at the same time. A green-painted concrete area is hardly a sustainable alternative to a lush green lawn in a home environment; alternatively a lush green lawn is not a sustainable alternative to a durable surface in an office parking area.

A few aspects to consider when selecting inorganic surface covering:

- Make sure the material is **practical** for the purpose. Select durable outdoor tiles for safe, non-skid surfaces.
- Select materials that are **in scale** with the intended project – this applies particularly to small, intimate areas, cottage-style designs and where a change in tempo might be desirable – like slowing down at a gate, viewing a special feature or approaching an important entrance.

- Loose hard surfaces such as gravel, bark chips, pebbles or crushed brick pieces can be as effective as fixed hard surfaces, especially in areas where there is **less traffic**, but they often tend to have a 'softer' user-friendly appearance which some designs require.

- Although plants are generally less durable than any hard surface, consider them in areas where **low-key traffic** occurs. In this way the design is not segmented unnecessarily by bands of hard construction, although this approach is still ideal for maintenance pathways in large planted areas.

Finally, be bold and interesting when creating surfaces; combine plants with hard materials, consider materials that are not run-of-the-mill or are applied in less than obvious ways, and where practical be led by your own imagination more than by current trends.

Some examples of HLE – Hard Landscape Elements:

Brick offers numerous opportunities even when not combined with any other materials. Firstly there are bricks of various sizes and colours, such as standard bricks, paving bricks and some interesting larger bricks; alternatively, consider the nature of the bricks – rustic or stock, semi-face, wire-cut or facebrick. Most bricks have three different-sized surfaces, the end, side and top, and create different effects when these surfaces are used in patterns, whole or in broken parts. Think of the combinations any one of these surfaces can generate!

Stone is popular in numerous forms – natural flat stones used as pathways or stepping stones perhaps, but trimmed and cut to size along with slate and even soft slate or shale (once popular as 'slasto'), for the rustic 'ethnic' look of current trends.

Stone **cobbles** cut from granite and sandstone have great potential for detail. They also combine well with other materials and create interesting bed edging or dividers between various other elements such as plants, gravel or bark chips.

Sandstone has recently begun to appear in numerous forms, most of them a far cry from the traditional Victorian stone architecture, much of which is being lovingly restored throughout the country. It is being offered for numerous applications and as a polished flooring takes on a new dimension – but take care, it can be slippery when used in large-sized pieces. It's a very dramatic modern material in some respects and limitless options exist, from dry packed walling to grand formal stairways.

Top: Vary the texture of surfaces where practical as it makes the design more interesting.

Above: Rustic slate still has an element of old world charm if used in the right setting.

Left: A popular 'new' use of sandstone is wire basket gabion walls and garden structures.

Left below: A dry packed wall of cut and trimmed sandstone adds a feeling of age and 'country'-like charm to a design.

Marble off-cuts from the domestic indoor industry are being imaginatively used, but can be slippery near water or in large pieces. Used formally, marble can strongly suggest

Below: A novel permanent pathway created by cementing pebbles together – it takes time but the final effect is worth it.

Below right: The sizes and colours available make pebbles a very versatile garden element.

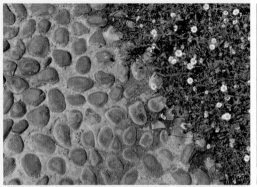

Wood railway sleepers have endless uses but do need oiling and termite treatment from time to time.

classic styles and conjure up ideas of statues and fountains ... but I don't see it as farm-style material!

Gravel, for some inexplicable reason, is only a recent addition to the South African garden, perhaps because there is an ever-expanding range of colour options as well as sizes now on offer. On the other hand, it could be that designers are realising that gravel is almost liquid in its applications, with endless design opportunities – and it's ridiculously inexpensive compared with other materials.

Pebbles have become firmly entrenched as a surface covering in the garden irrespective of whether the area (or the pebble) is large or small, and this is simply because they are so effective. They combine well with so many other garden elements, add detail where necessary, help create atmosphere whether the style is oriental or classic, formal or informal, and the range available is never-ending. Used loose on sand, plastic, trendy new weed control fabrics (even closely woven shade cloth will work well) or cemented in place, there is an almost organic 'feel' to areas where pebbles are used, while with other applications and combinations they take on a clean modern look.

Where natural stone leaves off, the imaginative use of **concrete** steps in. Modern technology in both casting and colouring has moved this product firmly into the twenty-first century – from bold in situ castings to convincingly cast 'stones', 'railway sleepers' or 'tree slices', not to mention the huge range of tiles with numerous applications. It is advisable to check for the quality of colour penetration if the product is tinted or textured because some of the poorer products only have surface colour and this will wear off with time. Remember sustainability – garden surfaces are generally expected to last a long time.

Long regarded as something best left alone, **wood** is one of the trickier elements to incorporate as a garden surface, prone to termite infestation, rotting, cracking and harsh weathering in the varied climates of the land. Technology has improved in leaps and bounds, however, and wooden decking has begun to appear more and more as a garden design element. Needless to say, there will always be the need to maintain the wood regularly, but there are more reasons to employ this element than to stay away from it. Because of its newness, professional advice should be employed if considering wood decking.

Used as steps, stepping stones or packed as a surface, the problems of **railway sleepers** are similar to those of ordinary wood, but old sleepers that are reasonably well impregnated with oil can easily be treated with further similar applications, making their life expectancy quite lengthy (but not everlasting). Off-cut sleeper ends or 'bricks' make an interesting alternative to more conventional paving, ideal for detailed areas or where an organic atmosphere is desired.

More natural wood and wood-like applications such as **chipped wood**, **wood bark nuggets**, **nutshells** or **fruit pips** (peach and cherry pips have been used very effectively), can be regarded as short- to medium-term 'soft or organic' effects in the garden and can be topped up or moved to other areas for renewed effect. Incidentally, they are an ideal surface under old established trees where plants and lawn battle to grow but where water is necessary for the well-being of the trees and alternative surfaces may be too solid, preventing water from soaking down to the roots.

Above: Detailed cast in-situ paving slabs add interest to an entrance garden.

Ceramics are generally available in the form of manufactured tiles of numerous forms and sizes with endless design opportunities. Tiles offering the rustic look of baked terracotta 'quarry' tiles – usually square and in small sizes – are ideal when a neat, tidy surface is sought after. Alternatively there are the colourful 'Italian' or Mediterranean tiles, which ideally provide the obvious European style, but tend to be hazardous and slippery, and the patterns on those of poor quality are inclined to wear off. Tiles generally need to be chosen with care from a durability point of view, but because of the huge range of textures and colours they remain popular for patios and similar applications and tend, generally, to blend in well with most other elements.

There will always be the once-off or 'avant-garde' items that find their way into design one way or another – and these could easily range from crushed safety glass, or recycled glass pieces, to stainless steel punch-out pieces, handmade glass or tile mosaic designs or in situ-cast stepping stones or paving slabs impregnated with pebbles, shells or personalised items such as names, quotations or old metal hardware. Generally such items are used to enhance a specific theme or to accompany a specific style of architecture. These may simply be whimsical notions of a designer or home owner – however, irrespective of their origin, if used sensitively and in keeping with the other design components; they truly earn their place in the design.

Above: An unusual paving has been created by cutting railway sleepers into 'bricks' and used as paving.

Obviously surface coverings can vary as often as the design allows for change, but it is advisable that the smaller the area being designed, the more limited the materials. Generally a limited range of materials helps build more pleasing designs, even in larger and more expansive situations. This is where the mood board helps – clutter is never a good idea!

Above: Metal lattice work is perhaps more versatile than wood but will require regular maintenance.

The use of wall mounted lattice panels adds interest – particularly while the shrubs are too small to conceal parts of the wall

Above: A concrete in-situ pathway wide enough to use for all purposes yet in scale with the design.

Walls or vertical space dividers

Plants cannot solve all garden challenges in all situations. Space, privacy and urgency are often the critical factors, and generally the answer is some form of vertical structure. In many cases the materials are similar to surface coverings but simply used vertically, so it is not uncommon to see bricks, stone, wood and metal in constant use. Other materials that are manufactured in sheet forms for covering purposes – such as fibreglass, perspex, sheet metal and stainless steel – can also be used. Finally, some vertical structures are manufactured specifically for a design or are prefabricated and can be used in numerous combinations to create walls.

Lattice or trellis is as a popular example of a semi-private screen application. Mostly these panels are constructed of treated timber; in some special instances, metal. Because these panels are manufactured in various sizes as well as a range of shapes their applications are limitless and they blend easily with other construction materials to create numerous landscape styles. Slightly less durable are woven mats or panels of various organic products such as split bamboo, palm fronds and sisal that have a decided rustic feel to them should the design call for such a finish.

Conventional walls are the most common form of separating spaces. What makes them unique is how they are finished off: rock, concrete or brick can be covered with stone cladding, smooth or textured plaster, coloured with paint or pigments added to plaster, topped with metal palisade inserts. Even glass bottles, wagon wheels and other items of interest have found their way into walls and screens. So long as the end product is sturdy, sustainable and in keeping with the rest of the design, it can be built from almost anything.

Changing soil levels in the garden may make retaining walls necessary. They are often accompanied by steps (which may lead to a need for pathways) and in some extreme cases handrails and further walling. Because of the amount of material they hold back these retaining walls may require civil engineering expertise: it is essential that professional help is obtained because of the dangers and cost involved should badly built walls collapse. Even on a reasonably low-key scale it is important to make sure that there is sufficient drainage behind these walls and weep-holes in them to prevent water and subsequently water pressure building up behind them, as this can simply push the wall over.

There are several makes of retaining wall interlocking blocks that are easy to install and can easily be concealed by using plants planted in between the blocks. These are available from concrete product manufacturers. A similar product is the planter/bank retainer construction, which much like any other level change retention system, automatically defines area spaces. Often, these structures are attached to and part of standard walls and other architectural aspects incorporating the level changes with elevated planting areas and space definition. Sunken areas within a garden would probably be dealt with in this manner. (Make sure there are weep holes in raised planters or they tend to become waterlogged muddy planters and if badly built can burst open with the weight of the water.)

The ceiling

Gardeners automatically think plants when they are considering a ceiling or canopy in the garden: after all, this is an area of live things. Often time is of the essence, however: perhaps privacy is required, or a parking area for a new vehicle – a newly planted tree will hardly be an ideal option if shade is needed any time soon. Over the last few decades 'ceiling' materials in the garden have advanced and robust, low-care materials are available. Pergolas – those frames, usually of varnished or treated exotic (hardwood) timber, supported on pillars, historically either brick or dressed stone, still have a place in the garden, however, and are an attractive means of growing and displaying creepers.

Prefabricated made-to-measure canvas and aluminium awnings attached to homes are increasingly popular, particularly those that can be rolled back or adjusted to allow more or less light in. Generally they provide an instant outdoor covered extension without the added cost and space loss of walls.

Equally popular in South Africa are 'lapas' in various forms. The name covers a number of structural designs, all generally constructed from saligna or gum poles, either treated against rot – as all outdoor timber should be, or varnished and set into or onto a cement base. The covering generally consists of thatch grass and this can either be fire-proofed or not.

Above: A traditional pergola still adds charm to a garden – where space allows.

Who said walls had to be boring?

Above: A creeper covered gazebo is an ideal setting to get away from the summer heat.

Below: The metal roofed gazebo adds a sense of Victorian charm to the garden design but requires some maintenance.

The designs and sizes of these structures vary almost with each new 'lapa' that is constructed – sadly many of them do not add anything other than shade to their settings. This is simply because not all garden styles will readily accommodate a rustic or semi-rustic lapa as a design component: careful thought should be given to this style of garden 'ceiling' prior to erecting such a facility in a design.

Fortunately there are many attractive alternatives to the lapa, making it possible to incorporate some form of 'ceiling' in almost any garden, irrespective of its theme or style. The gazebo is perhaps one of the oldest means of providing shelter in a garden, combining covering with a sense of being part of the garden. Generally these light structures incorporate either timber, or more recently metal, in whatever architectural style is required, creating an airy, open-sided structure that can be covered with canvas, slatted wood or metal, plants or shade cloth. Apart from those that are constructed to house creeping plants, the effect is usually complete in the time taken to erect or construct the gazebo.

A variation on the theme with closed-in sides has become known as the 'summer house' and generally refers to a structure a lot more substantial in all respects. Almost a small cottage in concept, the summer house is often designed and constructed with doors and windows, electricity and toilet, washing or change room facilities. Needless to say, this form of structure needs careful planning because services are involved.

Above: With a bit of imagination and clever design using high-tech materials – stainless steel and aluminium – gazebos can really be interesting.

Talking of simple garden structures that are expected to provide a form of 'ceiling', there is not much that can compete in effect and simplicity with an umbrella. Numerous designs have reached the landscape market of late and I am surprised how many gardeners turn to the simple umbrella only as a last resort. Various in form and size, hugely colour manipulative to meet the needs of any theme in a garden, they are easily opened or closed, stored, repaired ... and they are movable! In climates such as ours this is an important aspect as the open space is often used for a host of activities or people – depending on weather and season, a mobile ceiling is generally a good idea.

Slightly less simple yet easily erected are shade cloth structures, perhaps not resistant to all odds in the garden, such as hail or heavy snow, but cost effective when constructed of simple wood or metal frames and covered with shade cloth of a desired shade thickness, colour or appearance. Because the construction material and shade cloth are generally inexpensive and construction is usually quite simple, these structures are ideal if a more long-term plan is intended which may involve plant material or alternative structures at a later stage. Although they may not be the most desirable people-friendly structures, if the design calls for some form of plant growing structure this type of 'shade-house' is ideal and in most parts of the country will work better than a 'hot' or 'glass' house.

Lastly, a thought on any ceiling that is expected to accommodate plant growth such as creepers that will become large, intertwined and heavy. Make sure that the design of such a structure is robust and requires little or no maintenance. Try if possible to use solid, good-quality wood poles or metal cross-pieces; if a long-life, low-maintenance structure is anticipated, consider concrete lintels or pre-cast beams.

Above and left: The sheer versatility of an umbrella and a small gazebo has a lot to be said for its place in the garden.

Below: Thatch adds an 'unique South African' feel to this entrance garden and adding welcome shade too.

THE PURPOSE OF PLANTS

Up to now much has been said about the role of HLE in design and the need for caution when placing 'hard' items. For obvious reasons, they must be incorporated in the design before plant beds have been shaped, soil levels determined and prepared for planting and plants purchased and planted. Doing things the other way around generally leads to chaos and problems in the overall scheme of things – and most distressingly, plants are disturbed or damaged.

Needless to say, gardeners interested in designing their own outdoor space are mostly interested in filling it with plants. The obvious purpose of plants is that they are highly visual, living aspects of any design, providing instant texture colour and form, changing with the seasons while they grow and mature. The alternative roles chosen for plants are often a little more obscure and in many cases more long-term, such as helping to regulate soil erosion on a bank, reducing noise or the glare of lights, providing a wind break or channelling people, animals or vehicles, as a visually more appealing alternative to HLE options.

Irrespective of the reason for selecting a plant there are guidelines that the aspirant gardener or landscape designer needs to bear in mind to make the selection as successful as possible.

Above: Plants are in most cases used either for their texture or for their colour.

Plants chosen for screening must meet with the needs of the area in which they will be planted. Height and width are paramount – not too wide for the area and tall enough without being so tall that they obscure light. The plants should preferably be evergreen or lose foliage for as short a time as possible. The rate of growth is important, as the desired screen should begin to develop soon after planting. Tolerance to pruning, when required, as well as adaptability to varied soil types is important. The idea is that the plants should be able to care for themselves soon after planting which makes for low maintenance and helps to conserve water.

If the plants are to be used for a wind break, to screen light or hide unsightly aspects nearby, then density is important – plants with sparse growth or that are deciduous will be uneffective. Ideally these plant types should have solid growth right to ground level, or they will not effectively serve the intended purpose as they mature.

Plants that are selected for soil retention on banks, or in areas where storm water erosion is problematic, should have a low-growing, spreading habit with a good root system (preferably continuously rooting as the plant spreads). Here too, evergreen plants that cover the area as much as possible throughout the year are better than deciduous plants, especially in areas of winter rainfall where the soil may be more exposed to rain and erosion as the leaves fall off.

If the plants are used to direct people or traffic, make sure that they are quick growing, have dense, robust or stiff foliage, are not prone to breakage and if desirable have sharp or thorny growth. These aspects of the chosen plants help to discourage walking or driving through the plants, particularly while they are young and developing and during the time that the desired traffic flow pattern is being established.

Although evergreen plants sometimes appear to have more advantages, deciduous plants are equally important in a design because these are the plants that can be used where there is a need for warmth (sun reaching into leafless areas) and more light in the winter months, a change in the seasonal density, or to add visual and tactile interest at different times of the year. Interesting autumn and winter effects – foliage colour change, the bare shape left once the leaves have fallen, or the seeds, berries or pods that hang on the plants well into the winter months, are important aspects of what gives a landscaped space its personality and the ability to be a living extention of the whole 'home' space.

Above: Some plants are selected for their detailed effect at specific times of the year (right), while others are more for their overall yearly effect (left).

Remember that there are both evergreen and deciduous plants that flower at the height of winter, when there are not that many flowering plants in the general garden and they contrast dramatically with the harsh winter effects and colours of most of the inland gardens. *Camellia japonica*, flowering quince (*Chaenomeles japonica*), some proteas and ericas are examples. And there can't be many sights to better that of the spring-flowering deciduous plants that burst forth after the tardy winter months and herald – often before the leaves – the arrival of a new growing season.

Sadly the warm, subtropical coastal regions tend to lose out on this aspect of plant choice – subtropical plant material is generally evergreen, and autumn and winter pass by unnoticed. This warmth is not conducive to

Above: Hedges grown for privacy must be keep short enough not to cut out light in parts of the garden or home.

Lef: The beauty of a Camellia sasanqua *flowering from autumn into winter is eagerly awaited by many a cold region garden lover.*

Top: Warm shady places are ideal positions for the host of dazzling impatiens which can in mild climates be grown throughout the year.

Above: A hot, sunny position is ideal for the beautiful range of indigenous Osteospermum hybrids available.

Right: The drift of grey leafed Lavender is in complete harmony with the 'exotic' pink blooms of Chorisia speciosa – 'kapok 'tree.

the successful growth of the more temperate plant material, including many deciduous plants and gardeners are often disappointed by their poor performance when they attempt to grow them in areas that experience little or no winter.

The Western Cape and surrounds are the exception to South Africa's weather pattern, experiencing winter rainfall and in some areas severe cold winter weather conditions as well. Much of the deciduous European plant material – such as the spring-flowering plants and even some summer-flowering plants such as roses – flourishes and only behaves poorly during the dry summer months if watering proves to be a problem. The 'fynbos' unique to this area is wonderfully in tune with this weather pattern, yet sadly too few designers consider it when creating a reasonably trouble-free garden for this area.

It is important to know enough about a plant to ensure that it is correctly used in the desired design. Numerous books and magazines provide valuable information on plant performance but an urge to experiment with new or unknown plants is what will make the design interesting. Always try to find out the basic information required to keep your plants happy and attempt to allocate them to an area in the garden where these requirements can best be provided. Consider the need for sun or shade and protection against frost in the winter months, strong winds or harsh afternoon sun. Ensure that the soil is as good as it can be for optimum growth ... and remember *all* plants perform better if well cared for regarding pruning, feeding and other general plant care aspects.

Whether plants are selected simply to provide a 'green wall' or for their artistic potential, there comes a time when they need to be grouped together as important components of the whole design. This will be the case irrespective of their final purpose – functional or aesthetic.

The ideal combination of colours, shapes and sizes is balanced, visually appealing, uniform (no avoidable gaps in the planting) and adds a feeling

of belonging to the design. These effects are easy to obtain if a few basic guidelines are adhered to.

Know when a plant is going to provide its best effects, be they based on colour of flower or foliage, seasonal changes or colour provided from other sources such as pods, bark or berries. Identify the time frame of these effects – a few weeks in a season or a lengthy period of effect such as a winter/summer foliage colour change? Some plants such as roses have repeat effects during their flowering period; others simply have one flush of flowers or foliage colour for a specific length of time – spring-flowering plants for example – and who would willingly sacrifice having this splash of spring colour in their garden?

Consider the colour impact of various plants growing together – some plants totally overwhelm those growing near them in terms of how their colours dominate those of surrounding plants. This can often be the case where strong colours are combined with pastel or pale colours. Red and bright yellow can over-dominate other colours. It might mean that much fewer of these plants need to be incorporated in any planting to help 'balance' the effect of these strong colours among other less dramatic colours.

Some colour impact becomes less apparent or less dramatic during the evening hours, so if the design is to be enjoyed at this time of the day make sure that there is sufficient lighting or add other plants that appear to 'glow' in the dark – such as white, lime green or yellow foliage or flowers. Similarly try to avoid deep red, black or purple foliaged and flowered plants or ensure they are well lit or balanced with light coloured material – irrespective of whether this is HLE or plants.

The same thinking applies to plants that are selected for size, shape or foliage effects – too many large leaves or an overabundance of 'spiky' foliage will tend to overwhelm a design. Plants need to be grouped according to their various similarities (or their ability to combine harmoniously with other foliage types), coarse or fine foliage, the natural shape of the plant, leaf arrangement and natural density. This not only applies to the branch and foliage arrangement but to the spaces created between them as well. This varied grouping together of plants allows for a large pallet of plants from which to choose irrespective of the desired end effect.

When the plants are selected in such a manner it is quite simple to

Top: Use light foliaged plants in the shade to 'lift' dark flowers and foliage of other surrounding plants.

Above left: Even in a small bed, foliage and textures are important.

Above right: Avoid too many plants of similar form – here bold foliage would balance the over-use of spiky plants.

select any combination of plants required for any specific effect, style or ambiance. So if a selection were to be made to suggest a woodland effect, it is likely that plants with soft fern-like foliage would dominate, colours would be soft and tending towards green more than any other colour; the plants would all tolerate moist, shady conditions and in most cases would be evergreen. Similarly any particular theme can incorporate plants that will add to the overall effect. Remember the purpose of the 'mood board' – to gather together enough ideas from all aspects of gardening to make the final idea come true.

Plant selection criteria

Plants are assessed on three levels before their final selection for a specific position in a design.

Level 1: General plant criteria

Size of the plant at its final or mature stage. In some cases this may be a slow process ... but if left unchecked it will finally happen. Often plants can be kept in trim by pruning, but if you've set your heart on a plant that will eventually be too big for your space, regular replacement may be the only solution. This could be the case in very limited space such as an atrium or built planter, or where a specific detailed design is called for.

Colour. What is the plant's dominant colour? Which aspect of the plant contributes the dominant colour – flowers, bark, seeds, foliage, etc?

Environmental impact. What positive or negative impact will a plant have on the environment of the area in which it is planted? For example, positive impact – draws birds and other wildlife to the area; negative impact – becomes invasive and overwhelming or host to pests or diseases.

Seasonal contribution. How does the plant perform at various times in the year?

Shape. What is the mature or created shape of the plant?

Texture. What visual and tactile impact will the plant lend to the planting?

Level 2: Particular requirements – the role of each plant

Screening. This is a long-term, sometimes seasonal function. How effectively will the plant provide screening (deciduous versus evergreen), and how long will it take to provide the necessary screening?

Focal aspects. To what extent can the plant serve as a focal element in the design? For example, a protea or *Camellia japonica* would serve as a focal aspect when in flower in winter, *Acer palmatum* in autumn when the leaves change colour, while standard fuchsias or agapanthus are more focal in summer when in flower and oak trees in spring when the new foliage appears. These plants will repeat this effect each year at the same time and they can be relied on at a specific time each year to add extra impact to the planting. For example, clivias and mesembryanthemums (vygies) will always be associated with the arrival of spring or early summer and hydrangeas are not known as 'Christmas flowers' for nothing!

Seasonal impact and presence. What will the plant contribute throughout the year? If pruned during the dormant period, like roses and some perennials, will the planting lose some of its impact during this period? Neighbouring plants will have to be used to create sufficient impact in other parts of the design to detract from these areas at this time.

Harmonious capabilities. Do the plants selected collectively create a feeling of harmony, or does the planting appear disjointed? This is often caused by an incorrect selection or quantity of plants chosen.

Colour. Will the colour provide an impact at the right time of year, for long enough, and be bold enough to relate to other material used? Is further colour needed to enhance the colour that exists in the planting? For example, small amounts of dark red or purple flowers or foliage tend to be lost if mixed with larger amounts of dark green foliage. By adding red/purple flowering annuals seasonally, a stronger impact is provided.

Above: The rewarding colour of this verbena brightens up any warm dry spot – even in containers.

'Movement' in the planting. To avoid a static, never-changing effect, plants should be included which, during the seasons, provide extra effect, besides their general appearance. For example, the spiky, blue-grey, evergreen foliage of irises is enhanced by their late spring flowering. During winter, some ornamental grasses and conifers change colour as the temperatures drop, but revert to more conventional colours during the warmer growing season, and mesembryanthemum (vygies) are for the best part of the year a reasonably drought-tolerant groundcover, but come spring and they burst forth in a host of iridescent floral colours.

Top: Few plants herald early summer like the beautiful orange or yellow blooms of indigenous clivia.

Above: Nandina domestica *in its full red winter glory – the colder the better.*

Opposite page

Top: Plant forms and colours are important elements that must always be kept in mind.

Middle: A few dramatic plant forms in a planting can make the world of difference.

Bottom: Interesting plant forms and textures will always attract attention.

Above: An example of ideal plant choices – successfully incorporating appropriate HLE.

Right: An ideal balance between a mass of Echeveria and pebbles that are in scale with each other.

Above: An attractive low maintenance combination of pebbles and Trachelospermum jasminoides *–'star jasmine' under an existing tree.*

Right: Although not all these plants are indigenous their requirements are the same and this makes for easy gardening.

Level 3: Information relevant to a specific theme or project

Style or theme. This will often limit the plant choice to particular plant types (see Chapter 8 for more detailed information). Texture of plants is very often directly related to the style intended. For example, spiked plants can be used for desert effect or ferns and moss-like plants for a woodland effect.

Brief of area to be planted. This is based on the desired overall effect of an area.

Size. The size of the individual plant determines if one or more specimens need to be used to create the correct effect in a designated area.

Quantities of each plant used. This needs to be calculated with an eye to the balance between the various plant choices. The smaller the plant, the more may need to be planted. In this way none of the plants are overwhelmed by the others.

Scale / proportion. This is relevant to the space available and to the combination of plants. This will prevent overcrowding the area.

Need for detail. Will large, simple plantings be more effective, or is a more compact, detailed use of plants desired?

Maintenance. The level of maintenance, or alternatively, the need for low maintenance will be directly related to the types of plants chosen.

Plant requirements. If the growing needs, climatic tolerance and watering requirements are similar, the collective planting will progress positively. Do not group plants together that require different treatment and conditions (for example, a rose garden under-planted with a succulent type of groundcover, or aloes grown in containers along with plants that have high water requirements). Incidentally, this is a 'water wise' concept, which helps to control water use and enhance water conservation in the garden.

Planting

It's all very well discussing the right plants, their functions and how many of them will be planted, but at the end of the day, gardeners want guidance on how to plant the plants to create the effects that they want. What plants go where? How wide a planting area and how far apart are plants planted to achieve the final effect?

The proportion, size and shape of beds are mentioned in other chapters, but simply put, a planting space must be large enough to comfortably incorporate all the plant material needed or intended for the final effect. This is irrespective of the desired effect, the time it takes to mature and the rate of growth of the individual plants chosen. In some cases the limited space will obviously mean that planting spaces are smaller and the choice of plants will need to comply with these limitations. This is often the frustrating case in the narrow spaces between adjoining properties where privacy is important, unadorned HLE are not all that desirable and most of the chosen or recommended plants grow too wide. These exceptions to the rule are the great challenges for the home owner and often the end results surprise even the most versatile gardeners and designers with their ingenuity and imagination.

The more general garden or site scenarios have far less challenging situations. It's simply a question of incorporating plants – as per an ever-increasing wish-list of plants recently seen or read about – into sufficient planting space and still retaining an open living area for various user activities, such as lawn, paving or some other alternative form of HLE like gravel, pebbles, and so on.

Over the years I have noticed that the methods of planting plants into a prescribed area fall into several categories. The basic simple form is to mark out a planting area, generally against the boundaries, seldom wider than one to one and half metres, and progressively fill it, at random positions, with trees (with much of the tree falling outside the designated property where it is duly mauled by neighbours, municipalities or other service providers alike), shrubs that have no harmony with their neighbours, and perennials that will never be lifted and split (as they should be) and have come from family, friends and the local 'throw away' area nearby. These planting areas, either straight edged or 'scalloped' in some enormously time-consuming, high-maintenance, snake-like form, occur through the length and breadth of the land and are simply a means of having a few plants in an otherwise unplanned open space surrounding a dwelling. There is seldom any form or intention towards design and the hardest part of such a planted space is to mow the huge expanse of lawn on a regular basis – perhaps!

Top: As plants mature it allows for new plants to be planted under the canopy of the existing plants.

Above: Plants at various heights all live successfully together in a narrow space, still allowing for a walkway.

Anything after this is a step in a better design direction! Some gardeners start with a 'list', some with an ever-expanding collection of plants

Top: Specialised plants will require specialised knowledge and care to perform at their best.

Centre & above: A simple (centre) and a slightly more involved (above) design made easier by planning it first .

gathered from all possible sources, and in many cases with total working knowledge of each plant's performance and needs.

In the case of the 'list', the tendency is to place the desired listed plants in positions which will show them off to their best, tall ones at the back, medium in the middle, and so on. Generally they are allocated sufficient growing space, as this information is dutifully recorded at the time that the plant was allocated its place on the list. (In many cases all relevant plant information is listed, which makes the placing of the plants that much more simple and specific). Unfortunately, such plantings do not generally show much regard for the size or shape of the planting areas and the result can tend towards a display area rather than a harmonious grouping of plants incorporated within a design. A by-product of this form of planting is that there are often 'gaps' of space within the design for which there are no plants on the list, or there is not enough space for all the plants on the list and the plants are 'left over' once the area has been planted. In many cases the plant collection tends to bulge out over the prescribed growing space and grass dies off, walkways and paving disappear or are overgrown to the point of impracticality. An atmosphere of organised chaos ensues.

An alternative method is similarly frustrating when trying to incorporate plants, to scale, into a design. A series of circles depicting plants grown to their full extent are drawn to scale, next to one another, and then plant names are allocated to the correct-sized circle. Many of the circles will easily be filled with desirable plants and as is the case in most situations the designers begin to 'see' the overall effect – *except* that there are a few circles for which there are no plants in mind and the design takes on the effect of Swiss cheese – it is obvious that a plant or plants must go into that or those positions but no plant is ideal, available or known. The quandary is whether to leave the space open until the right plant is found or look for an alternative – often with disappointing results – not to mention the time lost in searching for the ideal plant.

An effective method that avoids many of these problems is a combination of the last two options, namely to know what the plant will 'do' in terms of size, rate of growth, and so on, *and* allocate it a position which will allow it to perform to its best – from the beginning.

There are several forms of this process employed by experienced gardeners or landscape designers and a reasonably simple set of guidelines to follow:

1. Identify the need for all the HLE first, paying attention to the relevant size, direction and functionality – this would relate to walkways, pool, sport facilities, patio, driveway, parking and service areas – in fact any of the essential inorganic areas, *even if they will only occur later.*

2. Decide the extent and type of open space required – more near a pool, sport facility, summer-house or parking area perhaps, with less in an area of communication or domestic function such as a wash line, garden shed or refuse area.

3. Separate the list of desirable trees from all other plant choices and identify their specific sizes, shadow path (west to east), and root systems (remember all services). Unless opting for a park-like effect, avoid allocating trees to lawn areas where they will with time cause the lawn to die off as their shade cover develops. Remember to keep trees away from areas beyond your control – neighbouring properties, municipals or government facilities (including the existing street tree plantings); this is to ensure that the trees are not wantonly pruned by others!

4. Identify areas for planting, remembering the analysis of needs in the zone or 'bubble' diagrams drawn earlier. Consider these areas with regard to their functions – screening, wind breaks, scent and or seasonal colour, areas of important focal impact and any other role the plants may be expected to play in the design.

5. List, from a preferred plant selection, plants that will create the major plantings and effects relevant to each of these positions, determining how many types of plants and quantities of each will be required to create the desired effect. In many cases simplicity of selection – a few well-matched plants – in larger quantities proves to be more effective than a large selection of individual plants – it prevents the 'botanical zoo' appearance. Don't be afraid of plant repetition: it

Above: Rooms-within-rooms in the garden are easily created by planting and maintaining hedges.

creates harmony and unity within the design. For example, a narrow space requiring privacy will be ideally suited to the use of a limited selection (even one) of tall narrow plants such as bamboo varieties *Nandina domestica* or *Freylinia tropica*, creepers or clipped hedge plants, to provide the ideal effect. The use of repeated containers instead of a planting area could further enhance the simple yet striking effect.

6. Once these plants have been identified and allocated their positions, material of a more seasonal, whimsical and supportive nature can be added to the list in areas where space or need arises. An example of this would be in an area where privacy of an area such as a swimming pool or summer house is essential but because the area is used either seasonally or more intimately than other parts of the garden the need for colour, specific plant forms or perfume are a

Top: Care and proper maintenance of any hedges is important or they can become too large or unsightly.

Centre: Seasonal colour will provide the best effect in areas that are seen or used often.

Above: Accessories should enhance rather than conflict with a design and often need only be placed later.

Top: If there are too many roots to dig a hole place containers in the bed and plant in these.

Above: In many cases the accessories won't look like much if seen alone and need plants for design balance.

Right: Shady areas allow the introduction of plants that could not have been used there when the plantings was new and the area was sunny.

desirable extra, over and above the need for privacy. Similarly, areas of minor importance with regard to their initial function – plants along a path or driveway, for example – can be enhanced with colour or focal aspects to enliven the area in general.

7. Because all plant lists, either written or memorised, seem to contain an element of changeable material such as seasonal colour and other short-lived plants as well as perennials, seasonal bulbs and various other seemingly unimportant yet desirable, disposable or movable plants, it is ideal to constantly have areas within the more structured aspects of the design where these plants can be employed – often to create another 'feel' in the area or enhance the plantings in a more informal, less static manner.

8. Remember to allow space for perennials to expand and continue to flower, since overcrowded specimens often stop flowering. Anticipate lifting, splitting and moving most perennials every two or three years – maybe to other parts of the garden for a revitalised look. However some perennials – hellebores, clivia and peonies, for example, don't like to be disturbed too often and it's a good idea to research this as part of their initial planting requirements.

9. At this stage, think about adding accessories to enhance the planting schemes. Consider containers, furnishings, umbrellas (for instant colourful shade) – in fact anything a garden space could require for the total effect. If need be, repaint containers and refurbish other garden furnishings to add new zest to young, undeveloped areas, or alternatively to pep up old tired areas.

10. By now it's important to consider how you will enhance your planted effect by cutting back out-of-hand plants, removing poor results or adding new material (or simply more of the happily successful plants). Always allow for this, because a garden need not be static: there should be space for new, yet-to-be-introduced plant material. This may be all that is needed to add a new angle to the current garden atmosphere – and maybe even change the style of things altogether!

11. Finally, as the areas develop the increased shade that the maturing plants provide will change the growing environment, creating shade where once there were reasonably long sunny periods each day. Remember that as the shrubberies develop, so too will their collective root systems: adding new plants may become a long-term challenge. In this case plants

grown in containers either above the ground or set into the ground may be a solution. Consider also the options that the changing environment offers – an opportunity for new plant choices that the original planting scheme could not accommodate.

STYLES

'Ye olde English', ethnic African, medieval, hi-tech, industrial or country are all styles, and gardens of the world have been following in the general style of things for centuries. Some are influenced by fixed structures or architecture – imagine a medieval castle set in a 'bushveld' garden! Mind you, the chances are that a lapa would look as uncomfortable surrounded by a stylised 'Tuscan' garden.

So what is this 'style' buzzword all about? Perhaps it needs to be simplified, in which case it is the intended visual atmosphere or 'look' anybody creating a garden hopes to achieve, on a specific site, in harmony with other structures and items of influence. These items could be architectural or botanical; in other words, existing plants have as much chance of influencing a garden style as fixed structures do.

An informal style might be found in a well-laid-out park or surrounding a home on a larger property or farmstead. These styles lead the visitor easily from one area to another, through well-balanced plantings, down pathways, across lawns, through arches or pergolas briefly touching on water features, paved areas or plant collections with little or no indication of where one area begins and another ends *(see photos right)*. All the necessary attributes required for ideal use of the area seem to blend casually with each other, leaving the user and visitor with a feeling of a garden that is well planted without following 'rules'.

Highly formal styles give a manicured and stylised impression of mathematically measured botanical architecture. They leave the user in no doubt as to

chapter 8

Top: Formality generally calls for plants matched in size and shape.

Centre: This sweep of Bulbine frutescens is reminiscent of a veld situation – away from it all!

Above: Themed styles are often designed to comply with the name of the complex or resort such as this 'Bali' theme.

Right: This 'bonsai' and pebbles are typical of what one would consider as an oriental style.

where to walk or drive, and by doing so passing, turning or ending at exact points of interest. In these types of designs every aspect seems to have been designed and placed meticulously, right down to the matched plant sizes and shapes, perfectly groomed, almost without a leaf out of place.

Many styles fall between the two options and one of the fun aspects of design is determining where to start and end a design to suit the purpose and yet have visual characteristics of its own. Again, there are no specific rules, although guidelines do become more exacting as the design tends more and more to a specific theme.

Points to consider when considering a specific style:

- Look at the architecture of the structures for any trends that could influence the tone or theme of the surrounding layout. This is particularly the case when the property has been designed with a particular appearance or 'name' in mind, as is the case with many cluster housing and sports resort developments.

- If in doubt as to which direction to follow, make use of the mood board concept to assist – at least in compiling the HLE, colours and accessories. Plants have a way of fitting into most styles – unless the style calls for particular plant choices specific to it – indigenous, woodland, desert or oriental themes, for example.

- Pay attention to current trends and available materials. Plants as well as accessories move in and out of fashion and some older design books or ideas may not be easily reproduced with the identical components that were used when that effect was designed. However, innovative use of more up-to-date items can certainly give an old idea a new look.

- The expression 'not being able to see wood for the trees' readily applies when creating a design style: often the obvious is overlooked in an attempt to create something new and exciting. Pay attention to the simple aspects of the design while considering the style intended so that the end result is not hugely impractical, using a host of elements that could have been left out. Don't lose sight of the four all-important words – colour, form, texture and density (read through the principles of design again for good measure) – and apply them to all aspects of the style intended. This way, complicated, pointless pitfalls will be avoided.

- At the outset, list all preferences as well as dislikes: after all, the end result has to comply with the needs of the end users! Consider the user-friendly aspects of the surfaces, water ways, seating areas and so on, and if a slight 'bending' of the style guidelines is needed to fit in with a specific lifestyle – well, so be it. The style is being created to assist with an atmosphere that must serve up a large helping of personal satisfaction, and not to conform to any rigid standards.

- Take time in collecting the plants and HLE materials to create the best interpretation of a style possible – understandably the white sands reminiscent of some Mediterranean beaches will not come from 'the source'; neither will a sphinx, an authentic Dutch windmill or a 'host of golden daffodils'; even fynbos has its limits! But the more effort that is put into authenticity, the more realistic the end result will be. Consult, compare and refer again and again to the mood board, remembering that at the planning stage any design is simply thoughts on paper and easily rectified or changed – but moving wrongly placed boulders, uprooting dozens of plants or rebuilding a water feature is another matter.

- There is nothing wrong with collecting ideas from other people, visiting their gardens or gathering together pictures and photos of interesting aspects of a style. Take time out to visit, discuss and compare thoughts and ideas with other designers, specialised growers, home owners or experts in fields such as water features, garden structures or urban wild life. It all becomes 'grist to the mill': the final style will be none the worse for a bit of careful and dedicated planning to begin with.

Above: Don't forget the mood board when collecting accessories - mistakes are easily made and often physically hard to rectify.

Below: Well-built water features are a beautiful addition to any garden but expertise is called for.

Top: Existing structures often set the style of the rest of the design.

Right: The simple formality of this design has lasting appeal.

Far right: The inclusion of a 'classic' element often serves as a centrepiece for a formal design.

Below: An informal style will still employ all the necessary elements to make it successful, such as colour.

Style terminology

Firstly, what is style? Quite simply, this is a form of design that accentuates an architectural format in such a way as to expand the feeling of that format or theme into the remainder of the property, or it is a way of creating specific historical or international themes as part of an overall design, such as creating a classical or ethnic garden in such a way that they will provide usable pleasure to the occupants and/or users.

A **formal design** generally has an imaginary line through the centre, with all that is designed on the one side of this 'line' or axis mirrored on the other side. All components are formal in nature, with straight lines, exact angles, whole or part of exact circles, and even numbers of plants and accessories – unless they fall on the 'line', in which case one may be employed, e.g. one central water feature. In most cases, the area in which these designs are created is formal, and if not, then it is planted so as to provide an open central formal area within which the design is created. Styles that fall within this rather exacting form of gardening are classic French gardens, knot gardens, gardens reminiscent of the Renaissance in Italy and more recently, the South African version of 'Tuscan' architecture!

Typical of these styles would be clipped hedges, in various heights and textures, very stylised garden structures such as obelisks, balls, cones and numerous examples of classic containers, gazebos and colonnades or statues equally classical in appearance. These styles tend to be rather static and are generally demanding in terms of maintenance. Should a plant die it is quite difficult to replace it with one of similar size or appearance. Generally these styles are kept to smaller areas and are a particularly successful method of incorporating herbs, vegetables or roses into otherwise less formal gardens – particularly if they can be screened off with hedges or trellis walls.

An **informal design** is generally quite the opposite to anything formal. The success of such a design is created by the balanced use of plant material – dark against light, a few large plants against many well-chosen smaller ones, a balancing of natural plant forms, and so on. In many of the more successful attempts at informal landscaping there is a feeling of rooms within rooms, each one inviting the user to ramble on to other parts of the design. Plant quantities are generally in odd numbers, and unlike the open 'stand and see it all at once' of the formal garden, colours, forms and textures are used to invite the user to move on into the garden and experience it phase by phase.

There are numerous excellent examples of this almost timeless style in South Africa. Most of them consist of relaxed, flowing lines, easily maintained and home to numerous plant combinations, changing with the seasons, and full of opportunities for experimentation. Care has to be taken when using this style in areas too small for easy flowing shrubberies, as it tends to take on a rather cramped appearance, and simply using alternative smaller plant material does not always work when related back to the standard size of the conventional structures such as buildings or doorways.

Above: A well balanced albeit informal planting stays a pleasing part of any design.

Geometric styles could be said to be a very convenient way of combining the above two styles. They are often a combination of the flowing casual lines of the informal style, harmonising with the mathematical precision of the formal styles. It was gardens designed in this style that gave birth to the brick or concrete mowing edges, textured surfaces of driveways, raised planters, patios

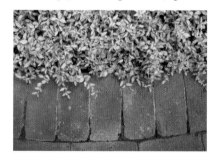

Left: An elevated view of a pleasing geometric design.

Above: The well maintained hedges add a geometric feel to a reasonably small area.

Far left: Brick mowing edges – an easy way to keep a garden in trim.

and other informal seating areas in the design, as well as the geometric pond and pool shapes and expansive use of groundcovers and other groundcovering methods to replace the vast expanses of lawn. Ideally suited to large and small areas alike, this style offers a host of expressive opportunities that neither of the previous two do.

Dramatic containers simply planted with equally dramatic material expressing a form of minimalism have become an increasingly popular

if not extreme form of this design style. The expression that 'less is more' has never meant so much to the landscape design fraternity as it does now. No area is too large, or too small, for an interpretation of this design style, and the plant growers and accessory suppliers have made sure that the sky is the limit when it comes to choices.

One enjoyable aspect of this style is the increasing use of architectural form plants, which once established (having been provided with all the right requirements), will grow to enhance the situation with little or no fear of the plant demanding high levels of maintenance. That is – if the right plant was chosen initially, of course!

Ethnic styles are those that are typical of a specific country. Oriental or Zen gardens, English country gardens, designs typical of Mediterranean islands and architecture of the palm-filled gardens of some tropical region such as Bali are all typical examples of this form of garden theme. They require research to achieve plausibility, taking into consideration such local aspects as climate, soil types and plant choices available.

There is a growing awareness of South Africa's own ethnic possibilities. Indigenous plants, accessories such as containers, furniture and garden ornaments fixtures and structures (here I grudgingly go as far as to include a 'lapa'), have become more and more popular, particularly when used in conjunction with Afro-tourism – game lodges, holiday resorts and housing developments. Once again there is an increasing use of architectural plant forms such as aloes, grasses, appropriate palms and other plants easily identified with the ethnic theme or style intended.

Above: Plants such as these Cycas revoluta, *which come from Japan can easily set the style of the garden.*

Top: Change the water feature and accessories and the overall style of the design would change too.

Right top: Many ethnic styles call for specific accessories to complete the ambiance.

Right: Indigenous thatch reed Chondropetalum tectorum *and stone easily impart an afro-ethnic theme.*

Opposite page bottom right: For a relatively low maintenance garden style there is quite a popular move towards more natural gardens, favouring indigenous plant material and often readily encouraging extensive wild life too.

Experimental styles tend to encompass those that may or may not have a reasonable sustainable lifespan. I have heard terms such as 'industrial', 'hi-tech' and 'eccentric' to describe the styles that are emerging from this design genre. Generally the HLEs dominate – stainless steel, chrome, Perspex, glass, mild steel and a host of other industrial-type materials feature quite prominently. The design lines are quite clean and uncomplicated, plantings are dramatic and often minimalistic, and the trends seem to be geared towards very low maintenance yet optimum impact. There is an increasing use of crushed stone, as opposed to gravel or pebbles; sandstone is being employed in dressed as well as semi-natural forms, and accessories vary from mirrors or stained glass to mosaics and plastic products. The effects are dramatic but time will tell if plant-loving designers are happy with such an increase in one aspect of the design options to the detriment of another.

Above: A man-made 'natural' water garden encourages a whole host of wild life.

Top right: Styles such as this are generally trend-based and often short lived needing constant attention to keep them looking good.

Centre right: Pebbles repeatedly occur irrespective of the style – perhaps because of their versatility.

Environmental-styled areas are another reasonably new approach to landscape design, with a strong emphasis on the environment, even to the point that the design tends to take on a natural (or 'shaggy-dog') appearance rather than a 'designed' one. Lawn will blend with planted areas, often passing through areas of 'wild' grasses and into the shrubberies. Water features may move through natural filtering eco-systems of selected plants, culminating – if space allows – in a 'bog garden' providing feeding and nesting havens for wildlife. Generally the emphasis is strongly towards indigenous plants, with plantings carefully selected to conserve water – grouping plants of similar water requirements together and trying to emulate the natural order of plant groupings where possible. This concept has popularly become known as a component of 'water wise' gardening.

As this is a reasonably naturalistic approach there is the chance that the tidy-minded gardener who enjoys the order of all the plants in their right place may find this form of style a little too rustic to live with on a daily basis, but again there is a growing tendency to adopt this style in areas where space and ambiance allow it to be developed to its most effective end result. It certainly has rearranged the concepts of colour, form, texture and density, and gardens designed in this style are interesting if only from the point of view that they tend to dispense with so many of the standard concepts of design as they are known. 'Dry riverbed'

approaches replace conventional driveways and walkways are often small trails among clustered plantings of strange and unknown plant specimens, while wild life often abounds with the human participants taking a back seat to the nesting, feeding and daily (and nightly) activities of birds, bats, bush babies, hedgehogs, reptiles and insects of a range hitherto unknown in many urban gardens. Words like 'boma' have replaced the more conventional patio, selected 'veld' grasses are desirable plants to collect, lawn mowing has been replaced by gravel raking, goldfish and koi are replaced with shoals of tilapia, and bird feeders have made way for food-bearing plants for the birds or other inhabitants – in many cases the wildlife is as important as the plants. The guidelines are decidedly in favour of the environment: once they have been put into place a whole new world awaits the adventurous designer.

Top: Even in a limited area an afro-ethnic theme can readily be accommodated.

Right: There are no holds barred when it comes to creating a style but try for consistency.

Below: Raised planters make it much easier for the elderly and disabled to garden.

Accessories – well chosen make a dramatic style statement.

Whimsical garden styles usually cater for a specific group of users such as children, disabled persons, the elderly and users with a specific passion – say a 'fairy' or a herbal garden for example. The guidelines in these styles are generally prescribed by the needs of the users: plants with scent and texture for the partially sighted; raised planters for disabled or elderly gardeners; plants that can be harvested regularly for the herbalists – traditional or otherwise; pathways that consider the disabled, with low gradients rather than steps or extra wide for wheel chairs to pass each other.

Generally such styles dispense with the more conventional aspects of a designed garden unless there are specific needs for an element to be included – lawn for children to play on would have meaning for children but not for a herbalist who wants optimum plant space; and an abundance of colour would have little meaning for users who could not see it, so each of these styles would prescribe their needs before commencing with the design.

A mood board in such a situation may have more to do with identifying the specific needs of the participants than with the finer detail of aspects such as furnishings or accessories, but this doesn't imply that such a styled garden space is uninteresting or without the visual or tactile enjoyment of other types of styles – in fact there is often a greater challenge in creating a garden with a purpose than there is to simply 'making' a garden.

Rooms within rooms. A satisfying environment may in some instances be able to house more than one style without it looking out of place. This approach, known as 'rooms within rooms', is quite typical of many home gardens where the limited space has to provide styles typical of several family members' needs and still have an appearance of having been designed as a whole.

Careful planning of how each area is screened off from others, bearing in mind the need for communication and a sensible maintenance pattern, will allow almost any space to have a multifunctional design. It is also not a bad idea to introduce a long-term aspect to a young garden, as the needs of the various occupants may change with time. This might include added parking as children grow up and more cars appear; extended seating areas in the garden as the family circle expands; conversion of the 'wendy-house' to a tool shed or outdoor storage space as the years pass, and the sand pit to a pond or compost-making facility when the patter of little feet have passed. Or a calm area for the elderly, family members or visitors as time marches on. So many things change with time: do not see the design of a garden style in any space as a static 'never-to-change piece of real estate' – rather see it as an opportunity to add and take away plants, HLE or garden accessories, enabling you constantly to be challenged and enjoy the stimulation of designing your own space.

Below: There will always be somewhere where the intimate quiet area can be created for a bit of privacy.

Bottom left: Whatever you fancy remember, the space is yours so enjoy designing it.

Bottom right: Perhaps a simple bench set in a cool shaded part of the garden is quiet and intimate enough.

75

ACCESSORISE AND PERSONALISE

Very few gardens are the same shape or used in the same way – so even though your space may have some aspects in common with others nearby (a growing reality as the cluster or townhouse phenomenon grows), the need for individuality in the design continues to influence how the space is used.

This leads me to encourage the designer to think a little 'out of the box' when it comes to interpretation and application of the various aspects of a design. Obviously it is rather difficult to encourage or train or trim a plant into being what it is not! Groundcovers won't become trees, and lawn will always need mowing, but there are aspects of a design which can be utilised to create a level of individuality using the same components as everybody else.

Needless to say, the mere fact that the end users' needs are different, family sizes and ages vary, and financial opportunities differ, will allow each designer to approach the design from a different perspective – but at the end of the day there are only so many options available with which to create the design. There are just so many plants and HLE to choose from and so many ways that they can be treated, and this is why I have spoken at some length about different styles, referring repeatedly to such aspects of design as mood boards and client requirements in the hope that the aspirant designer will enjoy the sense of adventure that designing a personalised space will offer.

Understandably, most keen gardeners will wish to create a well-designed space using plants as a dominant element – and at the same time not forgetting to create opportunities for adding further plants in the future, remembering that no design is a static event. The fact that plants grow bigger, wider, denser and more interesting with time makes any landscape design an ever-changing marvel (not that the marvels are always as planned – but the element of surprise is all the more reason to enjoy the design element of a garden).

So if the basic components are somewhat limited, how does one create a landscaped space with character? Simply by looking beyond the conventional and seeing the potential in other elements, processes or items that will help this design become unique.

Let's have a look at the HLE aspects of the design first. As mentioned previously, they generally fall within the categories of surface materials, wall claddings or walling alternatives, containers, specialised features such as water features or planters, furnishings and garden or landscape accessories – but it is how these elements are combined that makes them individual.

Unless money is not a major factor, most of the hard landscape materials used in a design are purchased as prefabricated or completed items, or the structures made from them utilise standard manufactured products, and in most cases they are used as intended. Consider for a moment alternative standard materials with which to create the same objective, and the range of options extends way beyond any designer's wildest dreams –particularly if you look beyond the accepted garden ornamentation items and start looking elsewhere for that particular item.

I have in the past scratched around old buildings being demolished as a marvellous source of wrought iron gates, dressed sandstone blocks used as foundations and ideal for steps, rustic seats, and low dry-packed walls (often complete with moss and weather patterns). I also pay regular visits to scrap metal heaps – some of my most interesting wall ornamentation and fun water features were salvaged from a scrap metal heap near where I live, and the dump sites of old farm implements are an endless source for that item – rusted farm implements, leaking milk churns, steel wheels, plough sheares (they are great for braaing on) and so

on. In many instances these highly individual items come from the most unlikely sources, such as mines and defunct fairgrounds as well as the gardens of large properties being redeveloped as cluster or townhouse projects.

Of course, old scrap items are not the only source of materials to give the garden an extra level of uniqueness; new everyday items used in a less conventional manner may also afford opportunities to put the home owner's personal 'stamp' on the design. And don't overlook an

Top: The out of the ordinary, like this water feature, personalises your garden.

Above left and right: Rustic seating created from old sandstone foundations adds charm to a shady nook sometimes coming complete with its own moss and ferns.

Left: A few bits of rock and some copper piping and the options are endless – a water feature that is very individual – every time.

Opposite page: Scrap metal pieces could add just the right touch to a garden theme!

Above: In some cases, such as with this water wheel, the skills of outside experts needs to be called in.

opportunity to have items made especially to suit your needs.

Consider also the finish of everyday aspects of the design – how the entrance or boundary walls are treated or painted, and what finish is given to old, revitalised containers or furniture and fittings.

I honestly believe that half the fun of creating a personalised aspect of the design is the underlying motivation. So, when next you sit on your patio wondering just what it is that is missing in your design, don't simply rush off to the local garden centre to buy a standard stock item – look beyond what it looks like now and envisage what it can become.

The same can be said of plants, in a slightly different way – I am referring to the standard approach that designers tend to have, placing all the taller plants at the back and gradually working forward and down to the shortest plants at the front. Plants have no idea if they are the 'tall' or

Above left: Adding interest to boundary walls can add individuality without excessive maintenance.

Above centre: Gates can be so much more than simply closing an entrance – they are the entrance to your world.

Above right: Think twice before you throw something away it could add just the right touch!

Bottom left: Everyday items can, with a bit of imagination, become a very personalised aspect of your design.

Bottom right: It might not have a very long life but such a wood sleeper water feature will have visitors talking.

'short' ones: an interestingly alternative atmosphere can be created by introducing some taller (perhaps specimen) material near the front of a planting, viewing beyond to what is planted behind these plants by looking under rather than traditionally over them.

This concept affords an opportunity to create small 'cameo' plantings or effects in a garden where an item of particular interest – a rather interesting sculpture or piece of weathered wood, a dramatic specimen plant or a little water feature which at other times could be overwhelmed and out of scale – is framed by the more general planting.

Another aspect to consider is that of maintenance versus the conventional concepts of how a garden should or could look. The popular concept is that anywhere that is not filled with plants or driven over has to be planted with grass, irrespective of whether anybody ever uses it or not – though admittedly somebody walks over it quite regularly, generally behind a lawnmower! But this hardly seems reason enough to have planted large areas of grass in the first place. There is the school of thought that would imply that at least 80% of a garden should be given over to lawn, but I cannot in my wildest dreams imagine why, other than to work harder than is necessary at keeping it cut short.

Regard the entire garden as an area with design potential and consider that there are some areas where other grass types could be incorporated – ones that need mowing less often, perhaps creating a 'meadow' feel to some areas – much like a small-scale version of a golf course 'rough'. Who knows, it could even encourage some golfers to stay at home a little more, while at the same time providing a food source for some wildlife. There is currently an upsurge in the use of indigenous 'veld' grasses in swathes in a garden for this very purpose. Alternatively there are areas that need have no grass at all and this covering can be replaced with one or several alternatives such as gravel, wood or bark chips – even, in smaller areas, with peach, cherry or plum pips, or seed pods (I have even seen grape seeds used to a great effect at a wine farm in the Western Cape). These 'other' surfaces afford endless opportunities for the designer to create levels of individuality while reducing the all-too time-consuming aspect of maintenance.

Another labour-saving opportunity that also allows for individuality is to replace the popular well-dug and trimmed edge with some form of bed edging, which in fact serves the same purpose! In the case of alternative surface coverings there may not be a need for a bed edging

Above: Bed edging is supposed to reduce maintenance, garden right up to it – there is no need for an extra edge.

Above: A purpose-made metal and stone bench – stacked with colourful cushions and you have the ideal quiet spot.

Right: A touch of pink! Perhaps a bit excentric but it will certainly liven up an otherwise drab area and get the neighbours talking – and it can be repainted as the mood changes.

Far right: 'What you don't fill with plants nature will fill with weeds'!

Bottom right: Containers – either planted or empty can add 'impact' even in a shrubbery – and they can be moved about from time to time to add further interest to other parts of the garden.

What you don't fill with plants, nature will fill with weeds!

at all, allowing the plants grown near the front to 'spill' out of their designated areas onto the adjoining surfaces. This approach is very effective in helping to create a natural, rustic or cottage type of garden and affords opportunities for detail. Imagine: nestled into these 'escaped' plants can be detail such as a group of interesting boulders, unique 'collectable' plants, small sculptures – maybe even a garden gnome! ... or low containers – not necessarily filled and planted.

What I am trying to get over to the hesitant gardener or landscape designer is that the space should be used to the full to convey or exude the user's personality, rather than dogmatically following what other people are doing. In this way you will be using a little more to create individuality than other designers have to choose from – and using it in a way that is unique to the architecture of the site and the personality of the end-user.

REDESIGNING AND REVAMPING

As I have said, no garden is cast in stone. At least in gardens that consist largely of plants, it stands to reason that as time moves on all or part will need to be re-considered. A new, young garden is generally a sunny affair, with trees throwing small areas of shade during the passing hours and seasons; but add a few years, and the shade begins to be something of a more permanent nature.

Add to this the changing needs of the home owners, and the situation becomes even more of a challenge. Parking areas are too small for all the family vehicles, some of the younger generation have moved out and in many cases some elderly have moved in, the swimming pool is a major nightmare and serious consideration is being given to filling it in or converting it into a koi pond. Perhaps there have been alterations to the home over the years and family focus has shifted from some of the old favourite spots to newer ones as a result. Then there is the age factor – the home owner may wish to enjoy more looking and less labouring in the garden space, or interests may have shifted over the years. Perhaps some specific garden activity now takes pride of place – growing vegetables, orchids, cacti or bonsai, with the rest of the garden left largely to its own devices.

Whatever the reason, there is a strong likelihood that at some stage the garden will scream out for some drastic attention to help put it back on track. Don't be led into thinking that this is purely an 'old garden' scenario, far from it. There is always that odd spot in the garden that has never quite been what you had hoped for, or the need to add that dream element has been postponed for years because of lack of funds, space or incentive. All in all, there

Top: The rest of the garden may take a back seat if a special interest gardening takes hold.

Above: Specialised garden hobbies like growing vegetables needs added attention and knowledge.

Finding 'new' garden hardware is as much fun as finding new plants.

comes a time to reconsider what you have and re-channel it into a new direction.

First, let's consider the difference between redesigning and revamping a garden space.

Redesigning is when the style of the garden space is to be changed: out with old and in with the new! Perhaps recent trends appeal to you, or simply the inexplicable need to 'do' something different. It might be a concerted effort to conserve water, develop an all-indigenous garden, or create a garden style that is easier to maintain.

Revamping involves a major tidying up of the existing garden, cutting back plant material that has got out of hand over the years, removing plant material, and to a lesser degree some outdated HLE – old slasto driveways and pool surrounds that are past their best and no longer contribute much to the garden space come to mind.

Guidelines

A step-by-step method that works quite well is as follows:

- Make a thorough assessment of all relevant garden hardware – paving, walls, old water features, sand pits, defunct play equipment or play areas, existing patios or driveways – in fact anything that is not easily removed and/or due for an upgrade. The reason for this is that although the intention is to redesign or revamp the area, some of this existing HLE may be incorporated or at least covered over rather than going to the effort or expense of having it removed.

- It is a good idea to check the state of existing services at the same time – corroded water pipes or ineffective irrigation systems, for example, and if there are any outdoor electrical power points it is not a bad idea to have these checked as well.

- Pay attention to the state of wooden and metal HLEs; rust and rot have a way of creeping up on the unsuspecting and the replacement effort or cost may be avoided if a thorough cleaning and preventative treatment is applied at this time.

- This is an ideal time to consider investing in new or upgraded garden hardware such as furniture, containers, umbrellas or ornaments to introduce a new – and not necessarily expensive – atmosphere into an otherwise unchanged area. Paint, as discussed in the previous chapter, can work wonders and with modern technology some of the effects that can be achieved make old items as good as new. Alternatively, simply by moving the containers into new positions, adding some new plant material to the containers that have outgrown their effectiveness, adding a few other accessories along with the  containers – some boulders, a piece of sculpted wood or some pieces of steel (rusted or otherwise), a swathe of gravel and an interesting edging of some form or another – and voilà! – an area takes on a whole new look.

- Now consider carefully what plant material is to be removed, remembering that once well-established material is removed there is seldom a second chance – generally it cannot successfully be replanted to try and repair an 'oops'.

  Pay attention to aspects such as how much more light and sunlight the area will get once the plant or plants are removed. What effect will this have on the plant material you wish to keep? What will happen to the levels of privacy that have developed over the years, and what vista, good or bad, will be re-exposed?

  Consider the fact that some plant material has a limited lifespan and all the feeding and care in the world will not prolong its life to any great extent. Proteas and other fynbos plants, some Australian flora and several really fast-growing trees such as keurboom and Cape silverleaf are notorious for this. It is a good idea to find out the lifespan of such plants and, depending on how old they are, take the necessary steps now rather than be sorry later.

Above left: New plants and new positions for existing pots offers untold new options.

Above: By adding a few extra accessories such as a piece of drift wood can effectively 'lift' an old area.

Below: Although sword fern Nephrolepis exaltata *is a category 3 invader weed if you have it in the garden you may keep it – just don't distribute it.*

- You may consider getting acquainted with the list of declared and invader weeds, and decide that now is as good a time as any to take them out. Some are allowed to remain while they are alive (these plants are referred to as Category 3 invader plants – such as jacarandas or loquats; Category 1 plants *must* be removed immediately). There is comprehensive literature on these plants available from most botanical gardens and the relevant government departments. See lists at the end of the book.

- Having earmarked – note, *not* removed – the unwanted material, consider the state of the remaining material. Does it need to be cut back, and to what extent can this be done while ensuring new growth off the remaining plant material?

  There are many plants that will tolerate a light and regular cutting back or seasonal pruning, but react violently when they have to undergo a major cut-back – many plants such as lavenders, rosemary, 'daisy bushes' and some proteas and ericas are typical of

Top left and right: Cut back Lavender and May bushes often to prevent them from becoming woody, untidy and short-lived.

Above: Prune spring flowering plants such as this Cherry soon after they have finished flowering

this predicament. It is always a good idea to make sure that there will be sufficient foliage on the plant once the cutting back has taken place – rather cut small amounts off regularly and only cut again once the new growth begins to develop and matures, rather than beheading the plant in one fell swoop! Other plants prefer to be cut back at a specific time of the year, rather than when the mood comes over the gardeners! And then there are those spring flowering plants that if pruned too late (near the winter months) won't flower next spring, simply because the flowering wood has been removed – these plants, if pruning is necessary, should be cut back just after they have flowered and in time to produce new flowering wood for the next season.

- There may be plants that you wish to move from one place in the garden to another. Although this does not apply to all plants (the evergreen plants are the most tricky) I suggest that you call in the assistance of a professional horticulturist or landscape contractor, or at least seek advice as to how and when to undertake this task. In some cases, really big material such as some trees and palms, moves reasonably well, while almost all Australian and many South African plants don't move well at all, irrespective of how young they appear to be.

- Finally this is the point when removal, cutting back and moving of plants can begin. To soften the blow slightly, it is also a good time to begin compiling a list of proposed new material – unless you already have a list so long that you could revamp or redesign all the gardens of all the homes of all your family and friends and still have plants with nowhere to go!

- Consider this – the roots of all the plants that have been growing in any one area have over the years compacted the soil to an almost solid mass and so the next step is to thoroughly rework the soil. It is pointless to try and remove all the existing plant roots of plants that are chopped out, but if the area is to undergo an extensive make-over, which may include paving or water features, it is a good idea to remove as much of the underground material as possible

– particularly of plants that tend to regrow from the stump. I am not a great believer in using herbicides (plant killers), but I would suggest that you enquire about the likelihood of regrowth at this stage rather than pay a belated price.

- Should the revamping of an area necessitate the introduction of extra soil, bear in mind that many trees will not tolerate excessive changes in levels of the soil surrounding them. A solution to this is to pack a 50 cm wide collar of dry bricks, rubble or rock against the trunk – something that can expand as the tree girth expands, to the height of the intended new level; alternatively, at a safe distance (30-50 cm) from the tree's trunk build a small retaining wall and leave this 'well' surrounding the trunk empty.

  Similarly, should the upgrade call for the removal of soil surrounding an existing tree, and subsequently the removal of roots, a sturdy retaining wall needs to be incorporated on the design at a reasonable distance from the trunk of the tree. I would opt for a double-course wall the same height as the excavation (it can double up as a form of seating, perhaps) at least 2-3 metres away from the tree's trunk, so that when new roots develop there is space for them within the walled space. Further care must be taken not to compact too close to existing trees if the area is intended for paving – and contrary to some practices, do not add a layer of herbicide or plastic under the paving. There are open-patterned blocks available that can be packed in the immediate vicinity of the tree allowing for the movement of moisture through to the root system.

- Your new space may take some getting used to, so it is a good idea to spend some time checking out the new micro-climate – is it hotter, windier, or more exposed to the cold?

- Take care when selecting plants not to make the same mistakes again with species that grow too big, have a limited lifespan, and so on: consider this a golden opportunity to investigate the possibility of using plants (and HLE) that you are not familiar with. If the redesign or revamp is on a scale you are not familiar with – from a large garden to a small town-house property or visa-versa, take time to study up on plant material more ideally suited to the new venture than the same old plants that you have dealt with for years.

- If a drawn design is called for or you feel that you would rather take the time to experiment on paper first, try where possible to pinpoint all the remaining (existing) plant material as well as HLE (see notes on triangulation in Chapter 2), and pay particular attention to their shade movements. Unlike a new garden, the remaining plants will

Above: Try some new plants like these beautiful indigenous Scadoxus multiflorus *to revitalise parts of the garden.*

Below left and right: Look for smaller or different forms of the plants rather than those you have always used such as this small leafed holly – Ilex dimorphophylla *'Hollywood' and* Spiraea japonica *'Little Princess' mixed with ground cover roses.*

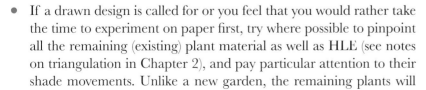

Top: Plant a splash of seasonal colour – like the lobelia used here, to lighten up an area that does not flower very often.

Above and top on opposite page: When revamping or redesigning it is an ideal opportunity to install a prefabricated water feature or a specialised fountain.

Right: A make-over can offer an opportunity to resurface around an old pond with one of the many new options such as wood decking

Opposite page

Centre: Consider building the water feature above the ground where roots will have less of an impact on the construction.

Bottom: Consider the root congestion when planting under existing plants, and prepare the area well prior to planting

have a reasonably well-established shadow path and adding the wrong new material in these areas could lead to some frustrating moments.

- If parts of the area are to be re-established with lawn, enquire at a reliable lawn-grass supplier what lawn would be best suited to the area, particularly if the growing conditions have changed drastically to the previous conditions (more shade, much hotter, retains more moisture, and so on). Again, this is a golden opportunity to consider some of the 'newer' lawn types – particularly if the area undergoes a change in its use pattern. You might consider dispensing with lawn altogether, in favour of some of the more interesting alternatives, such as mulch, gravel, bark or wood chips or even nut shells.

- Redesigning a garden space offers a not-be-overlooked opportunity to add new aspects to the garden. Bore-hole, irrigation system, outdoor lighting or other electrical points are all items that generally cause unacceptable upheaval in an established garden and as a result they are often put aside waiting for the 'right moment' (which as a result seldom if ever happens). Make use of this once-off opportunity to add all the aspects that will make gardening all the more enjoyable as well as reducing labour and perhaps long-term costs.

- Don't miss the opportunity to enhance an area of the garden into the otherwise dark night hours by utilising one of the various forms of garden lighting. Always employ a qualified electrician!

An interesting specimen plant can be lit from below using 'up-lighters', an intimate seating area could be enhanced with a form of low-level floodlighting (even consider the use of colour – nothing over the top – a soft blue or green, perhaps), or spotlights could be used to draw attention to a special feature within the areas most used – a water feature or garden sculpture, for example. The opportunities are endless, and as a garden matures there will be numerous situations that could be emphasised by introducing lights. If at all doubtful or curious, consult a specialist in outdoor lighting as to what options there are.

- Similarly, if the makeover is seen as an opportunity to introduce some form of ornamental water feature, such as a fountain, reflection pool or something on a more grand scale, consult a reputable pond or water installation expert. Issues like electricity, pump size, water flow rate and water volume can make the project a resounding success or a dismal failure. Plan the concept thoroughly, considering falling leaves, reduced amounts of sunlight (perhaps), root systems and other hazards that an established garden may present.

There are many innovative ways in which water can be used, from a relatively small feature near areas of activity at the front door or near an outdoor living area to something more grand and spectacular, so don't miss the chance – particularly if the younger family members have all grown up and mishaps are unlikely.

It is also a good idea in areas where there are established plants and resultant root problems, either to design water features that are very shallow (after all, in most cases it is the surface and above that creates the impact), or to construct the entire feature above ground, relying on a solid foundation to give it its stability.

- While considering major changes, don't forget that it is often equally effective to simply rearrange the movable plants in the garden. Lifting and splitting of the more common perennials not only allows them to flower better – I think of such rewarding plants as irises, day lilies, cannas, agapanthus, clivia and red-hot pokers, many of which are left year after year until they not only stop flowering well (or altogether), but often become overshadowed by other larger plants and serve little or no purpose at all. By reconsidering their positions, perhaps adding a few newer varieties and replacing some with alternative plant material more suited to the current conditions, a tired, neglected area of the garden can take on a whole new lease of life. What's more, the amount of work it entails in the bigger picture of upgrading or revamping is negligible (and usually quite cost-effective too).

All things considered, redesigning or revamping a garden is simply a means of changing an existing garden space – how it looks, lives and grows, to regenerate the interest, accommodate some flight of fancy or fulfil a dream. And because each space is different in all respects, the sky is the limit when it comes to choices. But don't be hasty, there is no point in making changes that leave you with a feeling of regret. Any atmosphere in a garden takes time to develop and can be irreparably destroyed in a short space of unplanned time.

As with all aspects of landscape design – when in doubt, hesitate, and never be afraid to seek professional advice. After all a few rands spent wisely once in the planning stages, can prevent the cost of many rands and years of lost time at some later stage.

A last thought on any form of revamping – try not to lose sight of the fundamental basics, consider the architectural aspects of the property, make sure that any changes are sustainable, by using quality products and correct plants, and make sure that the site is properly prepared *before* any construction or planting.

THE COST OF THINGS TO COME

As with all things, there is probably a distinct line between what you would like to have and what fits the budget. Designing a garden is no less of a financial challenge, and the final design may owe more to budget constraints than a whimsical wish list. However, until the needs are costed with some measure of practical reality, it is difficult to gauge just how much all or any part of the project will cost.

You may, of course, limit your designs to what you can do yourself, or what you can afford to pay a professional contractor. A word of caution at the outset, though – it is wise not to over-capitalise on your property regarding landscape projects in relation to the area you live in, as there is the chance that you may not be given credit for all that your garden has cost you in the event of resale. But if you are going to undertake this project simply for the sheer joy of

Above: Decking needs maintenance and expert installation, but has a very user-friendly impact on out-door living areas.

living in a pleasing space I strongly advise against considering the cheap and often unsustainable alternative. This is particularly the case with regard to basic site preparation and when constructing the hard landscape aspects of the design.

It is not essential to have all the money at hand at once; any project can be undertaken in a series of stages extended over a period of a few years if need be. However, it is wise to identify important aspects of the design that need to be tackled first and make the necessary provision for these elements in the early construction stages. Do this before adding any of the finer detail, which may cost less but will be disrupted when major works are undertaken at a later stage. Once the design phase has been completed, contractors can be approached for a costing of the project or various aspects of it and funding can be raised through home loans, banks or other similar institutions.

Considering the options

Irrespective of how the project will be funded, it is essential to do a costing and formulate a feasible budget. It is not a bad idea to consider alternative options and make a 'plan B' – when considering materials or plant sizes. For example, the surface treatments for seating areas, pool surrounds or driveways offer a host of alternatives, some costed at rates per square metre. Greater or smaller areas can be costed accordingly – don't lose sight of realistic scale of such areas though (see Chapter 4), while others, gravel for example, are costed per cubic metre and depending on what thickness is laid down the cost can rise or fall quite considerably. A cubic metre of 19 mm gravel, spread 75 mm thick, can cover up to 13 square metres – a reasonably good investment!

Keep in mind that there is often a price difference when ordering small **quantities** of some materials. In some instances minimum quantities apply, which can have a considerable impact on the costing of a project. Often the materials will only be delivered onto the pavement, with devastating effects on whoever has to cart it into the property! Consider too the delivery costs of the plants or construction materials, and if you live in an out-of-the-way area or the site is a difficult one to access, check with suppliers before ordering as to what extra costs can be anticipated.

Talking of moving things, remember that **labour** is an expensive commodity, and even unskilled labour can constitute a considerable portion of the costing of any project (unless the unskilled person is you!) How long will it take to do it personally, particularly if you anticipate learning how to do the work as you go along? Remember there is nothing more expensive or time-consuming than having to do things over due to inexperience. Consider asking for a quotation from a professional landscape or building contractor.

Although it is safe to assume that there will be considerable **savings** if projects are undertaken 'in-house', I suggest that you restrict yourself to the tasks you know that you can handle and employ the services of experts in the more specialised fields such as electrical installations, providing an effective irrigation system or building facilities that are expected to hold water without leaking.

Always ask for **references**, and get more than one quotation before accepting any price. Remember, to safeguard yourself at all times, make sure that all quotations are given in writing, dated and refer to a company or a contact person and the specific project to be undertaken.

If the project quoted on has been designed by you or on your behalf, make sure that all parties concerned with any aspect of the design's development confirm that they fully understand what it is that you

Above: Though not that fashionable any more, rock-work is still an ideal way to retain a bank – if built properly!

Many new paving options are on offer but use professional people to install or lay them.

Above and right: When mass planting, look for plants sold in mass quantities or which can be separated quite regularly, its cheaper in the long run.

Sloped areas are best planted with instant lawn to begin with to prevent erosion.

require of them before commencing any work, and that you have this assurance in writing. Many unpleasant situations have arisen from lack of communication on landscape projects: this should be an enjoyable and exciting undertaking, so prevention is far better then any cure.

It is important to understand a little of **how plants are costed** and what to look out for when buying plants. I do not hold with buying plants from street corners or anywhere other than reliable plant sale outlets where the plants are well cared for, properly named and in good growing condition. Always insist that the plant has a name tag to help you

identify it when it has arrived on site, especially if – as with roses or agapanthus, for example – you need to know what colour their flowers are going to be.

In the past some trees and shrubs were sold in winter 'ex open ground' which meant that they had little or no soil around their roots – this was common practice with dormant plants such as roses and fruit trees. This practice has all but disappeared and all plants, bar a few very large tree and palm exceptions, are sold in some form of container.

The cost of trees and shrubs – including individually containerised perennials and ground covers – is based in part on the size container they are grown in, whether a 4, 10, or 20 litre bag or plastic flowerpot. Larger specimen material will be grown in containers up to 100 litres. Generally these and larger containers (some in excess of cubic metre crates) are extremely cumbersome and considerable forward planning is required when contemplating their use in a design. Some plants do not grow well in containers for an extended period of time, or they are so fast growing that to produce them in larger containers in impractical – these plants are generally only found in the smaller containers.

Plants that are generally used in quite large quantities, such as groundcovers and perennials, are often sold in multi-cavitied trays or 'packs', although there is an increasing tendency to grow some of the more interesting or unusual plants as individuals. The price of the plants grown in such trays will depend, in most cases, on the size of the trays and the number of plants in them.

Don't waste your money: make sure that the plants purchased are

in all instances well grown, few or no roots are growing through the bottom of the container and that there are no tell-tale signs of them being root-bound – roots growing above the soil, old, weathered and torn containers, faded or no labels and a general appearance of a plant lacking good colour and putting on new growth.

In most cases today lawn is sold by the piece (usually 50 × 100 cm in size) or per square metre in the form of sods cut from lawn grass farms by machines, and is either laid as an instant lawn or broken up and planted in the more traditional method of rows of grass sprigs. The price of lawn sold in sod form depends on the variety of the grass, and in some cases the quantity purchased, and an additional cost should be added for delivery. In some cases the suppliers will professionally install the grass. Lawn sold as seed is increasingly common, but the varieties that are for sale are generally very site-specific – for sun or shade, to cover a certain amount of square metres or of a specific texture. It is advisable to enquire about all the relevant information before considering this grass planting method to avoid costly mistakes.

Most **hard landscape materials** are priced per kilo or per bag, for example mulch, pebbles, wood or bark chips, and some forms of compost or gravel. Such items as soil, gravel, bulk compost, sand, manure and crushed rock (as opposed to gravel of a specific grade) are sold by the cubic metre and costed at a collected or delivered price – but some do have minimum quantities. It is almost impossible to have 'set' formulas for these products unless the supplier can give some indication, because of the various sizes, and each sized item covers a larger or smaller area

Rocks are sold by the load or singly! Should you have an urge to build a rockery, generally 'dressed' sandstone or similar rock products are priced on the item required – some per square metre, others by a cubic metre or metric tonne.

Top left: Consider all building material options and costs when undertaking a building project.

Top right: Use inexpensive rugged materials as an alternative in areas where traffic is not that busy.

Above: When buying rock, try to purchase material that is in keeping with the area in texture, form as well as colour.

Other alternatives to organic ground coverings include items such as paving slabs and the material such as sand on to which they are placed, pebbles in the right sizes, quantities and appearance (colour or texture), as well as gravel, or other soil covering material such as nut shells, bark or wood chips and the products on which they are laid – either weed-controlling fabrics, coarse sand or a cement screed (depending on the final application). These products may be costed per square metre delivered, or laid or collected by you.

Garden hardware like railway sleepers, paving slabs , lattice panels, picket fencing and other similar HLEs are generally sold per item, depending on quality, size, finish – painted or not – and so on. The more common forms of concrete or brick paving are sold as per square metre laid by a

Centre: Select solid wooden railway sleepers and treat accordingly for optimum lifespan.

Above: The range of concrete products is vast – buy quality and keep to one style in one area.

Right: Good quality wood products, well cared for should add charm to a garden for years.

contractor, but bricks or concrete paving material can be purchased by the hundreds or thousands – either collected or delivered – and in some cases brick manufacturers will sell 'loads' of broken bricks by the truck load. These are ideal for rustic paving.

Portable garden hardware includes items that are not design fixtures, such as containers, wall plaques or sculptures, lattice or trellis work, including wooden or metal-covered seats, arches, obelisks, ornamental spires, balls or topiary frames. All of these, as well as umbrellas, other garden ornaments such as prefabricated water features, bird baths, dovecotes, and garden or patio furniture, will generally have an off-the-floor price, and in some cases delivery will be extra.

The costing process

To help consider a sensible costing process, the following relates to any project, large or small, anywhere within the boundaries of South Africa. All information is subject to variations in local circumstances, suppliers, and contractors.

Professional fees would include such services as surveyors, architects, plans purchased from local authorities or the government printers, soil tests, the assistance of landscape design consultants or professional horticulturists. In most cases these fees are charged by the hour or as a percentage of the overall cost, although some consultants will charge per project.

Site preparation machinery may be needed for cutting and filling, removing rubble or bringing in extra rock or soil. These machines (usually with fuel and operator) are charged out at an hourly or daily rate. The services of tree movers, tree fellers, bore-hole drillers and rock blasters are generally costed per item, depth in metres or per project.

Earthworks include shaping, mounding, levelling and preparing the site to be planted or compacted for paving, and (in the case of pebbles or gravel) the use of fabrics to prevent or discourage weed growth. Much of this will be done by hand so an overall figure including labour, supervision and material costs is quite common.

Where there are banks that need retaining using bank retention products or in extremer cases 'hydro-mulching and seeding', expect to be quoted per square metre or per project.

Earthworks also include the artistic and careful placing of rock or in-situ boulders and engaging the use of machinery with which to do this. Remember that one- or two-people sized rocks are not really big enough to create anything other than a spotted effect in most landscape projects. (A one-person rock is one that can be handled by one person, and a two-person rock is one that needs an extra pair of hands!) In most cases a project price excluding the cost of materials is the norm. It's anybody's guess as to how large boulders are costed – some developers are only too happy to dump them off-site, if you are in the right place at the right time, while other developers 'see you coming' and heavens knows what cost is attached to those rocks!

Construction includes the building of any garden components such as walls, brick mowing edges or simple bed or product dividing edges, steps or ramps, ponds and paved areas. Major specialised works such as tennis courts, swimming pools, 'art-rock' constructions or summer houses, lapas, pergolas and gazebos are generally quoted for off a plan (which if drawn for you is charged for) – make sure that they are municipality approved if this is necessary before work commences.

Bulk composting as well as fertilising or introducing soil that has been mixed with manure or compost for filling raised planters or adding a cover layer in areas where there is little or no reasonable soil – for terracing, for example, or to cover particularly rocky areas – are charged per cubic metre or minimum vehicle load or collected by you.

Installation of added services might include such items as French drains, irrigation systems, outdoor electrical points – either single or three-phase – and bank retention systems such as dry-packed walling, concrete retaining blocks, brick work or in some extreme cases, bank retention, using poles or railway sleepers or wire basket gabions (wire

If stone work is to include steps and level changes, employ competent craftspeople.

Above: Make sure that any climbing frames or structure are well built to begin with.

Top left: Wall mounted metal work will still need to be repainted or treated from time to time.

Top right: Steelwork in the garden needs to be well preserved against the weather and checked periodically – especially if it stands on or in the ground.

baskets filled with rocks and stacked one above another). Labour, supervision and materials are generally the items quoted on, but can take on the format of each project or (less common) a daily rate plus materials.

Make sure that the means of watering the newly planted areas is up and running and, if this is to be done by means of hosepipes, that they are long enough and that the correct sized fittings and tap connections are purchased along with the hosepipes.

Because there are so many options when selecting a service that is to be incorporated into the design it is advisable to 'shop around' rather than buy the first item that comes to hand. I am thinking in particular of irrigation systems, with their nozzles, computerised timers, valves, piping and pumps for moving water, as well as gate control mechanisms and garden lighting. There are reasonably priced, efficient products, but there are also some cheap, poor-quality alternatives, and as these are generally not the type of item one intends to replace on a regular basis it is wise to opt for the best affordable quality. Again I cannot emphasise enough the importance of proper documentation indicating the make, capacity or style of the item and any guarantees that may accompany the item. Make sure that there is a date and contact number in the event of any mishaps – though if expert on-site advice is required there could be a consultant's fee or call-out fee.

Planting would include the cost of digging individual holes for shrubs, trees and other single plants and digging over any areas for mass planting of such items as groundcovers or perennials and annuals. It will be necessary to budget for specific quantities of compost and fertiliser for these holes and areas and, where advisable, for the covering of the planted areas with mulch. One can safely assume that each hole would consist of one third compost and two thirds good soil with an added amount of general balanced fertiliser per hole calculated at roughly 30 g per hole – that is 500 mm cubic. Increase the fertiliser as the hole size increases but don't overdo it – rather feed more later. When spreading compost or other organic material such as kraal manure it is ideal to apply a layer between 50 and 100 mm thick and dig it in to the depth of a fork. Fertiliser would be applied at about 30 g per square metre. Mulch is applied at a similar rate as organics

In most cases a contractor will give a blanket quote covering compost, fertilizer, placing, labour and supervision, but some will quote a price per hole. Obviously this price either includes plants as listed, as per plan or as per discussion. Insist on a list of plants and their bag sizes as well as a reasonable breakdown of costing if at all in doubt.

Next comes the cost of the plants in various bag sizes and quantities, including delivery costs, tree stakes and tree staking ties, where applicable.

Labour costs include skilled as well as unskilled labourers. How many people will be employed for the task at hand per day, and for how long? Consideration must be given to provision of transport or accommodation where necessary, as well as safety clothing or equipment such as gloves, boots or dust masks and protective eye wear if necessary. In most cases the norm is a daily rate excluding any materials, sometimes including transport if this a factor, but larger projects tend more and more to quote for the entire project, with some form of down payment.

If the project is to be undertaken by you then sufficient **tools** need to be provided for the amount of labour employed on the project – 10 people cannot share one wheelbarrow, for example. If you are hiring heavier duty equipment such as tractors and soil loading or moving machinery, where possible employ the services of the machine *and* the operator – but plan how many days you will require the machine for before you negotiate the price.

Sundries covers all aspects that crop up in the course of any project – those unpredictable but guaranteed-to-occur little eventualities, not the least of which will be sun-block or an umbrella, considering the fact that you are going to be working outside ... many frustrating moments are blamed on the non-cooperation of the weather.

When compiling this list for costing purposes I have assumed that at some stage during the design phase, all relevant areas were measured and that a fair idea of the required square or cubic meterage of all items was calculated.

Above: In areas where space is limited don't ignore the value of hanging baskets, but carefully select the plants used.

Below centre: Specialised garden structures should be selected with care and consider their lifespan and maintenance.

Below left: Although stone work seldom looks this way once completed but with time it will add an element of old world charm to a set of rustic stairs.

Below right: A simple wooden lattice arch frames and enhances a splash of colour on a blank wall and provides an ideal background for a potted topiary plant.

A well balanced combination of HLE and the correct plants can make for an eye-catching focal feature almost anywhere in a garden.

CONSLUSION

Well, my intrepid gardening friends, this brings me to the end of what started out to be a simple book on landscape design for the home owner. I did not for one minute consider it to be anything other than that. Because this was my intention I have tried to keep terminology simple and have avoided the common mistake of listing reams of plant names – that's what South Africa's many excellent garden centres and nurseries are for.

I cannot emphasise enough that the more you ask, the more you will learn, and if this is your first foray into the frustratingly wonderful world of landscape design I can only assure you that 'the more things change the more they stay the same' – in other words there will always be another answer to the same, many times asked, question. Should you ever get to the stage that you 'know it all', contact me – I will definitely be able to learn something from you!

It would be unfair to say that I did this all on my own, because I didn't. I have been encouraged by many, many keen gardeners over many years, all of whom were so willing to share little snippets of information with me. Oh! so often they allowed me to ramble through their spaces with my camera in hand, and at the cost of a cup of coffee or a glass of wine I came away so much wiser and richer for the experience. I doubt if they all even remember being part of my learning curve, but they were, and it has been eternally appreciated.

My deepest thanks go to some of my dearest gardening friends who allowed me to photograph aspects of their gardens, season after season. I think particularly of Sheila Green and her wonderful gardeners Jerry and Tim, Bets van der Merwe and Frikkie Bezuidenhout.

I would also like to thank a dear friend Christien Marx who read, often in haste, various chapters to see that I'd covered all the bases. And finally, the marvellous people at Briza, some of whom worked quietly in the background to put all the words and pics into a format that I am so thrilled with, particularly Hendali who managed the project – and me, so well: you're a star; and Christo for even allowing me to put over 40 years' worth of thoughts down on paper: your faith in me and patience are really appreciated.

After all, gardening is sometimes so fickle, that a little help from elsewhere is perhaps not a bad thing!

GLOSSARY

Annuals – plants that are generally germinated from seed, grow, flower, mature, set seed and die, all in the space of one growing season – i.e. summer or winter season.

Arbour – usually a small creeper-covered structure of wood or metal in a quiet or secluded area of a garden, generally large enough for a small bench and one or two persons.

Architectural style – refers to the style of architecture of the buildings and other structures on a property. It could be specific, historic, ethnic or modern.

Archways – generally narrow structured openings of either wood or metal or a combination of both that creeping plants are grown over, and are included in areas of the design where a partial vista is desired rather than a solid screen.

Areas – active – refer to the areas of a design generally seen as areas where recreational activities take place – swimming pools, tennis courts, play areas or multifunctional open areas.

Areas – passive – usually the spaces on a property allocated to planting of trees, shrubs and other plant material, and often separate various other areas in the design from one another.

Areas – service – a collective term for areas in a garden that are allocated to the numerous forms of essential activity – wash line areas, compost or refuse areas, outdoor storage facilities or parking areas.

Axis or centre line – an imaginary line that can be drawn through the middle of a formal design so that all aspects of the design on the one side of this line will be 'mirror-imaged' on the other side of it.

Bakkie – South African slang for a light delivery vehicle (LDV).

Balance – formal or symmetrical is a description of a design or part of a design that has both sides of an imaginary central line or axis identical or mirror images of each other. Generally used in classical designs which compliment similar architectural styles.

Balance – informal or asymmetrical is the alternative to the above form of design where there is no imaginary central line or axis and the various areas that make up the design are distinctly informal in application.

Bog garden – an area often adjacent to 'natural' water features where the overflow water soaks away into prepared or natural clay areas which are ideal areas for growing plants that need constant wet feet but a growing medium rather than the conventional water plants in a pond.

Boma – an ethnic African description of an outdoor area often enclosed by closely placed circle of upright wooden trunks or poles, which is generally used as an area with a place for log fires, casual seating and a general 'bushveld' atmosphere.

Borrowed landscape – an oriental concept where the design of a specific site or area makes use of and adds to surrounding landscape attributes such as tall trees or dense plantings to create a feeling of an area that is larger than is really the case.

Brick – the general term for numerous standard and specialised manufactured components used in building and paving. They are usually specific in size – 75 × 100 × 200 mm for conventional bricks and 50 × 100 × 200 mm for paving bricks, but there are variations. They are mostly made from baked clay or cement, but there are exceptions.

Ceramics – a clay product either baked, glazed or not, that are used to manufacture containers as well as various floor and wall tiles and the more conventional indoor fittings such as toilets, baths and hand basins.

Clay content – a term used to express the number of clay particles in a soil sample when soil tests are made. Generally the amount of clay in any given area will have a direct impact on the rate water drains through it – either slowly if the soil is very clayey or faster if there is more sand and less clay.

Climate – the general term for the behavioural pattern of all the weather conditions in any given area throughout the country.

Climatic requirements – the ideal weather conditions required by any plant to grow and perform at its best.

Cloudburst – the term for a typical inland storm, often in summer, when large amounts of rain fall in one area in a considerably short space of time.

Cluster or townhouse development the general term given to a development of homes that are reasonably close together, often with limited land available for gardening. In many cases these developments are enclosed by secure boundary walls with controlled and monitored entrances.

Colonnade – the term given for a series of columns linked together with a beam or beams. Used either in formal straight lines or accurately measured curves, they have long been a popular component of formal designs.

Communication routes – the routes through an intended landscape design designed to be used by pedestrians, animals or vehicles for the purpose of maintenance or to move from one area or structure to another.

Concrete – a reasonably flexible product created by combining water, cement, sand and crushed stone in various proportions, used extensively in the building or manufacture of numerous indoor and outdoor items from pathways and stairs to ponds and sculptures.

Concrete lintels (also known as pre-cast concrete beams) – the name given to reinforced concrete beams of various dimensions that are used to link various pillars, provide support over openings such as doorways, window spaces or many other forms of open archway – a pergola, for example.

Contour lines – lines on a plan that will indicate or link of all areas of equal height above sea level. They will provide information such as gradient, high and low-lying areas and river courses.

Dappled shade – a term used to describe areas that are shaded but rather than being a solid shade situation these areas are in partial moving shade as a result of trees or canopies which allow partial penetration of sunlight.

Deciduous – the term given to plants which lose all their leaves within a short or limited period at the end of each growing season (autumn) and are usually totally dormant and leafless until the onset of the next growing season (spring).

Design – sensory – implies that the design or any of its various components appeals to various senses such as sight, touch, smell or taste. This is of importance when a design has to fulfil specific needs such as those of the handicapped, elderly or adolescent.

Design – could be described as all or part of a landscape concept that is committed to paper as a drawn or illustrated means of visualising, planning and costing of any such concept prior to initial execution of the project.

Design elements – colour – refers to the application and incorporation of colour in all its forms in any whole or part design. Generally it would encompass all forms of plant colour such as flowers, foliage and other noticeable organic colour forms as well as the recognition of colour in all other inorganic design components such as gravel, paint, fabrics and architectural structures.

Design elements – density – is simply a description of the ability to see through or be solidly screened by the various components of landscape design, such as plants, screens or structures.

Design elements – form – is a term used to describe all natural as well as man-made plant forms as well as a general description of other components used. It generally includes the height and width as well as the overall visual impact of the item.

Design elements – texture – describes the visual as well as tactile components of any landscape design.

Design elements are four basic components used in formulating a landscape design and relate to plants as well any other design components which constitute a landscape design.

Design principals – 'guidelines' to consider when formulating any form of landscape design. There are several and these have been dealt with comprehensively within the context of the book under the headings:

Design principles – **balance**

Design principles – **emphasis**

Design principles – **harmony**

Design principles – **line**

Design principles – **repetition**

Design principles – **rhythm**

Design principles – **simplicity**

Design principles – **succession**

Design principles – **unity**

Design principles – **variety**

Design principles – **scale**.

Domestic gardens – the common term given to gardens surrounding conventional residential homes.

Dry-packed walling – a form of walling often constructed using rock/stones either randomly, trimmed or 'dressed' and constructed without the use of mortar or cement. Plants are sometimes incorporated in the spaces between building material.

Evergreen – the term given to plants that retain most of their foliage all year round, although in most cases there will be leaf-drop and new growth at one time or another during each given year of growth.

Exotic – refers to plants or flora (as well as animals) introduced to a specific area or country from another area or place of origin.

Fibreglass – a reasonably specialised human-made product which is used for casting numerous components both indoors and outdoors in the design sense. It comprises a liquid chemical resin that is applied to a 'glass-like' fibrous component and once is has hardened it takes on a glass-like quality. Ideal for casting such items as ponds, pools, sculptures and containers or furnishings

Filtration system – the term given to any purification system, which employs any form of filtering to remove non-essential particles and so clean or clarify the end product. In the landscape application this generally refers to water either in pools or ponds as well as 1al cleaning of natural water sources.

Fixed items or structures – components on a site that are generally perceived to be immovable, such as walls, dwellings, services and other similar objects.

Focal, feature or accent point – any item in a design that is incorporated for the initial purpose of attracting attention, emphasising an aspect of the design establishing an overall theme or mood or directing attention in a specific direction. It may be organic or inorganic or an artistic combination of both.

French drain – the term used to describe sub-surface drains, generally built of rock- or gravel-filled trenches which may or may not incorporate drainage pipes or drainage fabrics. Their purpose is either to drain waterlogged areas or remove water during a wet season from specific areas rendering the site more usable.

Frost – black – the phenomenon caused by below-freezing winds that blow at times during the winter months and damage sensitive plants by 'freeze-drying' them. In most cases the adverse effects are more severe than conventional moisture-related frost.

Frost – created when moisture freezes during the below-freezing hours of extreme cold in winter months. Generally more prevalent inland, it is responsible for much of the seasonal physical damage to sensitive or tender plants during winter.

Gabions – 'baskets' made from strong galvanised wire mesh which are then filled with rocks wired closed and stacked on top of each other or wired together in areas where soil erosion is a problem or could become a problem. They restrict the movement of soil and slow down erosion-causing water forces.

Gazebo – a semi-permanent structure used in gardens often as an alternative to an umbrella. Generally they are open-sided and the 'roof' can be solid or used to encourage the growth of climbers over it.

Glass- or hot-houses are structures once made almost entirely of wood, metal and glass for the purpose of growing special, exotic or sensitive plants that cannot survive in the more typical climatic conditions of any specific area. Nowadays many such structures are constructed of 'plastic' sheets and aluminium frames.

Graph paper – paper on rolls or sheets that are lightly yet accurately marked into millimetre and centimetre squares, which can be used to accurately plot aspects of a design and its various components such as structures, services and other relevant or important information.

Grass – sod is a way that many grass types can be purchased from some nurseries or grass-sod farms and installed for instant cover of an area. They are usually 1000 × 500 mm in size, which means two placed side by side will cover one square metre.

Grass – sprigs is a more conventional way of planting a lawn, particularly if cost is a factor. The grass runners or sprigs are planted in furrows approximately 200 mm apart, rolled and allowed to grow and cover an area.

Gravel – a general term for crushed rock of different screened sizes and colours used as a hard landscape option.

Hard landscape elements (HLE) – all items that can be or are used in landscape design which are regarded as 'inorganic' and can vary from concrete or paved surfaces to containers, sculptures, pools or ponds and numerous other items used to create a specific design.

Hard surface – a term given to surfaces constructed or cast from materials that will not generally deteriorate, referring particularly to such surfaces as those of some sports facilities, roads and parking surfaces as well as most forms of paving and pathways.

Header-course – a row of bricks placed side by side which usually serves as a reasonably stable edge to various forms of paving. In the case where the paving is dry-packed (not cemented together), the header course usually has a shallow foundation under it to keep it in place.

Herbicides – another term for all products manufactured that are capable of correctly killing weeds and other vegetation – more commonly called weed-killers.

Humus – an old term for the natural or added organic quality of soil – the less humus the less organic nutritional value the soil will have.

Hydro-feeding/hydro-mulching – the concept of mixing selected seeds, fertilisers and an 'adhesive' product together with water, in tankers or spraying equipment and spraying it out onto areas where revegetation is required, such as banks on new roadways, reclaimed open mine projects or coastal sand dunes.

Indigenous – the term used when referring to plant materials (among other things, such as fauna) that are endemic to an area or region. In the wider sense it will refer to plants that are specific to an entire country.

Kerb – either natural products built in-situ or precast, a kerb is the edging to hard surfaces, roads, some parking areas and garden beds.

Landscape design – a general term given to the planning of a man-made landscape surrounding, between or relevant to fixed structures, including buildings, roads and other immovable items for among other

things the purpose of beautification, environmental reestablishment or to create an outdoor, user-friendly area for passive or active recreational purposes.

Lapa – a South African name for an outdoor structure generally constructed from wooden poles, in most cases with a grass thatched roof, similar in function to a gazebo but more rustic in appearance. Open-sided or partially enclosed; wood slats are optional to the design.

Lattice or trellis – names given to constructed panels more often made from crossed or interwoven wood strips but occasionally of metal that are used for ornamentation, to screen or as a frame onto which climbing plants can grow.

Metal palisade fence – a style of fencing made of sturdy metal upright sections, often pointed or barbed, welded into frames or built in between brick columns as a form of secure yet 'open' fencing.

Mood board – the concept formulated to assist in compiling ideas or moods when considering creating a specific design style; a means of gathering all possible design elements together on a board to help visualise how they can or will be used together and what their combined effect will be.

Mosaics – a name given to small squares of coloured grass or ceramic that when bedded into cement or plaster are used as a form of ornamentation and design on walls, containers, swimming pools, or floors as well as numerous other applications.

Mowing edge – an edge installed generally between shrubberies and grass to prevent the grass from growing into the bed and allowing for easy maintenance of the bed edge. They can be constructed of brick, cobbles, cement, wood or any other impenetrable material. Thinner edges are usually made of plastic or metal but serve a similar purpose.

Non-garden areas – areas within a landscape design that are used for other activities or services as an alternative to using the areas for planting anything.

Non-skid surfaces – surfaces that will not become slippery when wet or worn; should be seen as important when providing surfaces in public places or areas of high activity such as patios, pool surrounds, pathways and ramps.

Obelisks – ancient stone pillars that are generally tapered towards the top; they are usually square, hewn from stone. They have been used as a form of garden ornamentation through several design periods and styles and are again regaining popularity although now many are cast in concrete to represent hewn stone.

Oriental or Zen gardens – garden design styles that have their origins in the Far East in places such as China and Japan; although popular world-wide they are truly perceived to be of a wider lifestyle philosophy, which can sometimes make it difficult to create the true concept of these gardens. Zen gardens generally make little or no use of plant material in the general context of the word, but selected sand and or stone are utilised to create a garden-like effect.

Pathways – communication routes that allow for access and passage, movement within or through a design for pedestrians or vehicles and can be created from a host of durable materials depending on their specific function.

Patio – also known as a **veranda**, **porch** (USA) or **stoep** (S.A.), an area attached to and part of a home that is in most cases roofed over but with open sides (optional) and is used as an extended outdoor living area of the home.

Paved area – an area covered with any suitable form of paving as an alternative to covering it with plants or lawn.

Pebble – see stone.

Perennials – plants that generally have a cycle of life through a series of seasons and live for several years during which time they will regularly flower and set fruit or seeds but will either die down at the end of each growing season or in the case of evergreen plants will tend to become shabby. They are then cut back and will generate new growth from the same rootstock at the beginning of the new growing season. They have a specific size that they will grow to each season and unlike trees and shrubs do not get progressively larger each growing season.

Pergola – a garden structure that usually consists of a series of brick or stone pillars erected in pairs with wooden beams across the top of them, forming an arbour or tunnel-like structure which is then used to grow creepers over.

Perspex – is the commercial brand name give to manufactured sheets of rigid coloured plastic, which can be used as screening panels as well as being moulded into containers and other interesting garden items.

Plant packs – are containers usually made from moulded plastic or Styrofoam that have been designed to hold more than one plant, much like an egg-box for plants.

Planter boxes – an American term for raised planting areas (raised planters) usually with sides only so that plant roots can extend down into normal soil areas.

Plaza – a term given to designed open public spaces within built-up areas, which traditionally would include areas for plants, lawn, paved surfaces and seating and tend nowadays to include areas for outdoor staged entertainment or places for public events such as music festivals or art displays.

Prevailing winds – the direction from which the more dominant winds move through any particular area.

Radius – the measured distance between the centre point and the outside edge or circumference of a circle.

Railway sleepers – although made of concrete, metal and wood, the term in a garden situation refers to lengths of various hard or exotic woods that were once used to hold railway tracks in position and are now available for various garden applications such as pathways, seating, steps, bank retention and abstract ornamentation.

Rain pattern – the term used to describe the nature of when (seasonally) and how (the type of) rain that falls in any given area.

Redesigning – when an area is completely redesigned, creating a new concept and generally making little or no use of any existing material.

Revamping – when an existing design is given a face-lift by removing ineffective components, retaining other aspects and using them in conjunction with new elements to recreate the area or its function.

Rhythm – either static, progressive or continuous – a design principle which enables the designer to include an element of visual and physical 'movement' into a design.

Rooms within rooms – a garden term used to describe a large garden space that has been visually or physically divided into small areas (or gardens) either by plantings or solid screens. These smaller areas often have specific functions or design themes.

Root-bound – describes the root system of a plant which has been grown for an extended period in restricting conditions such as a container. In some cases this will inhibit the proper and healthy development of the plant.

Scale – human refers to the size of all components in a landscape design and how they relate to the users of that aspect of the design, i.e. smaller for young children or large and dramatic in a public open space.

Scale – realistic measurement refers to the actual size an item needs to be to have practical and functional application, such as the width of a pathway or the height of a table.

Scale – the relationship between a realistic size and a proportionately reduced or increased drawing of the item such as a plot of land and its reduced scale plan. This reduction or increase is calculated in specific measurements such as 1:100, meaning the drawn item will be exactly 100 times smaller than the original but exact in every other way.

Screen – any way in which one area is closed off visually from another; can be created by using either HLE or plants depending on the level of privacy required.

Season – the time of year relevant to the growth of plants, such as summer- or winter-flowering or fruiting. It also refers to the four specific seasonal periods of the year – spring, summer, autumn and winter.

Seasonal change – the effect on plants, in some case visually apparent, as the year moves through the various months from spring to winter.

Services – all aspects of convenience that come into and exit from a specific site or property, such as roads, electricity, water, sewerage or refuse removal.

Servitudes – areas demarcated through properties or areas where service providers (municipalities for example) have access to sections of the property at any stage that they may need to upgrade or extend a communal service to; these services need to pass under, on or over that specific property.

Shade cloth – a reasonably non-biodegradable woven plastic cloth of various densities or weave-closeness, which creates specific percentages of shade for the purpose of creating shade on structures for controlled plant growth or recreational purposes.

Shrubberies – areas designated to the growing of plants collectively.

Site – a term for any area for which a landscape design is drawn irrespective of size. It would accurately include all components found on the area, such as existing plants, structures and services.

Site plan – the initial to-scale design drawn, which would include all relevant information as well as general proposals for future developments.

Skylines – another name for the horizon, but more specifically the close horizon seen from any property: surrounding buildings, other plants or open spaces.

Slasto – a popular South African building term for pieces of random-shaped and -sized soft slate or shale used in walling and paving.

Soil texture – the consistency of the soil in any particular position; refers to the percentage of clay and sand particles as well the humus content of a sample of that soil, when tested.

Step – riser is the height between two steps – usually 200 to 220 mm.

Step – tread is the width of a step for comfortable use – usually 300 mm.

Stone – the overall term given to a number of natural inert products, either in their natural forms, or naturally weathered, quarried or 'dressed' state; includes, gravel, pebbles, cobbles, and would include specific stone types such as marble, sandstone and granite among others.

Structures – a general term for all fixed constructed items on a site, such as dwellings, storage facilities, animal pens and the like.

Style – is an overall word used to describe the 'theme' in which the landscape is designed. It could reflect the traditional ambiance of a historic period (Victorian), atmosphere ('fairy garden'), 'concept, (formal or informal), country (Japanese), area (Tuscan) or race (African).

Summer house – this is usually a lightly constructed structure with lots of windows, open sides or removable screens that can be used in pleasant weather to sit outside in the garden away from the house.

Sustainable landscaping – this means that the design and the materials used have a reasonably well extended lifespan without undue maintenance and material replacement within a short period.

Tactile textures – those that can be felt as well as seen.

Temperature – the accepted standard temperatures for any specific area registered daily throughout the year between the maximum and minimum readings for that specific area, region or place.

Temperature fluctuations – the difference between the maximum and minimum temperature for any particular area or position at any given time throughout the year or particular season.

Triangulation – a measuring system which makes use of two fixed points to determine a third point in a triangular manner.

Utility or working spaces – another term for service areas.

Vista – the term given to what can be seen from any one particular position – they can be either pleasing or favourable, or unpleasant and undesirable.

Wood – a natural organic product derived mostly from trees (or some larger shrubs). It is classed as hard (quite durable) or soft (less durable) wood and is used in numerous forms in the landscape from its natural state, such as poles, chipped, bark nuggets, stepping stones (tree slices), to the man-made forms such as timber (lumber), boarding, or in its less obvious state such as nut-shells and fruit pips.

Zone or bubble diagram – a design process which enables the designer to visualise the positions of the various requirements within the overall design and allocate sufficient space to the various activities or functions prior to completing the final design.

ADDENDUM

Useful contacts

SALI   South African Landscapers Institute
www.sali.co.za

SANA   South African Nursery Association
www.sana.co.za

IPSA   Interior Plantscapes Association
www.ipsa.za.com *

LIA   Landscape Irrigation Association
www.liasa.co.za

ILASA   Institute of Landscape Architects – South Africa
www.ilasa.co.za

SANBI South African National Biodiversity Institute
www.nbi.ac.za

The Botanical Society of South Africa
www.botanicalsociety.org.za

MBA   Master Builders Association
www.mbsa.org.za

National Spa and Pool Institute
www.nspi.co.za

Department of Environmental Affairs & Tourism
www.deat.gov.za

SAGIC South African Green Industries Council *

* website under construction/not active at time of printing

Plant material planting hole sizes

Preferably all holes should be square/cubic and not round or cylindrical.

For trees and shrubs, depending on the size of the bag or container, I suggest that a hole twice the depth and twice the width of the container is dug.

For mass plantings such as ground covers or perennials the plants can either be planted in an area that is totally prepared to a depth of at least 20 cm or in holes a half again deeper than the bag and twice as wide.

Any sprigged or rooted cuttings that are generally planted in large areas an overall soil preparation to a depth between 100 and 200 mm will suffice.

Simplified metrification for the home owner

This very simple table will suffice to convert old plans drawn in any traditional imperial measurement to basic centimetres and metres. Old imperial house plans were generally drawn in eighths of an inch equal to one foot or sixteenths of an inch equal to one foot. Ie an inch on plan was therefore equal to either eight or sixteen feet:

1 inch = 2.5 cm or 25 mm
1 foot = 30 cm or 300 mm
3 feet (1 Yard) = 90 cm or 900 mm
10 feet = 3 metres or 3000 mm
100 feet = 30 metres 30000 mm
18 inches = to 50 cm or 500 mm (a half metre)

In most cases metric plans are drawn in millimetres *not* centimetres.

In some cases older construction books written in England or the USA will refer to all or most measurements in feet and inches, however more recent publications will either refer to metric measurements or include both imperial and metric measurements.

Many people still refer to property sizes in acres, half, or quarter acre and in some cases a third of an acre. Thus a quarter acre is equal to 1000 square metres.

A half acre to 2000 square metres and a full acre is equal to 4000 square metres and a 5 acre small holding is equal to 2.0 hectare or 20000 square metres.

Please note that these measurements are purely for general information and any greater level of accuracy required I suggest that accurate conversion methods or tables are referred to.

For liquid measurements that one might come across in overseas publications a general conversion is that a gallon of any liquid is roughly equal to 4.5 litres and if the article should refer to pints, then they are slightly less than 1 litre (Approximately 600 ml).

Similarly in weighing out of fertilizers an ounce is equal to 30 gm, a pound roughly a half a kilo or 500 gm and one kilogram is equal to a little over 2 pounds.

Interestingly enough in most cases an adult hand filled with granular fertilizer so that it can still close, will hold the rough equivalent of one ounce or thirty gram of the material. Test your self by adding a few hand-fulls to a scale and see how close you are.

The area of a **square** or an **oblong** is measured by multiplying the length (l) of the one measured side by the breadth (b) of the other measured side.

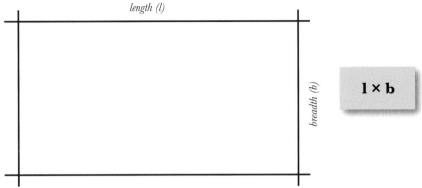

$$l \times b$$

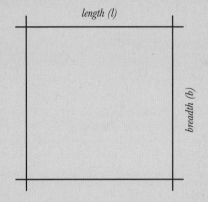

The area of a **triangle** is measured by multiplying half of the base length (½ l) (between two of the angles) by the perpendicular height (h) measured to the third angle.

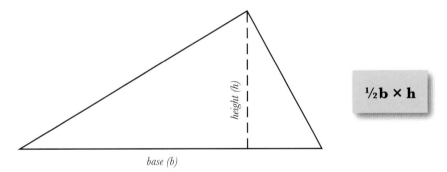

$$\tfrac{1}{2}b \times h$$

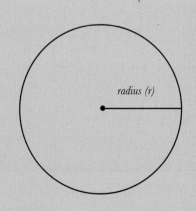

The area of a **circle** is measured by multiplying the radius (r) by itself and then multiplying the result by 22 and dividing the result by 7 (This is known as Pi and is written as Pi r squared).

Obviously for a half or quarter circle the result would be divided by either two or four respectively.

$$\pi = Pi$$

$$\frac{22}{7} \times r \times r = area$$

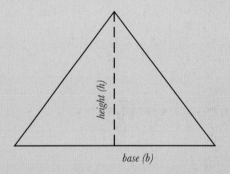

The area of a **cubic** item is calculated by multiplying the length (l) by the breadth (b) by the height (h); similarly a **cylindrical volume** is calculated by multiplying the base area by the height of the item.

Anything more complicated than this I suggest you consult experts in the field.

Passive areas would include shrubberies, areas for bird feeding, quiet seating areas, screening from neighbours or other more vigerous activities and places for specific facilities – i.e. outdoor showers, specific plant collections, private gardens off specific areas of the home such as main bedroom etc.

Active areas would include areas where specific or general forms of outdoor activity take place – pools, ball areas, play areas for children and pets and visitors.

Service areas are where outdoor space is required for activities which assist in the general running of the home such as deliveries, refuse removal, vehicle parking, outdoor storage such as garden sheds or washline or fuel storage areas.

Communication routes are those real or imaginery routes moving comfortably from inside the home into the property and from one area of the property to another for the purpose of maintenance and general convienient movement.

Focal points would be positions where an item of interest would be placed so that it enhances the area when seen from particular positions.

 = Focal point

= Areas of major activity

= Screen

 = Communication routes

Zone or bubble diagram

When creating a zone or bubble diagram for your house as explained in chapter 6 *(see page 47)*, keep the following in mind:

1. indicate the house on the property with basic relevant elements such as patios, walls, vistas, out-buildings, driveways, main entrances and exits from home and property;

2. identify service areas and parking areas;

3. determine areas of major activity for example the patio;

4. identify areas for passive activities – quite corners, special effect areas such as at entrance or parking areas;

5. position possible focal points as seen from relevant aspects of the home – view from patio, through bedroom windows or arriving and leaving through front door or driveway;

6. consider communication routes, where screening is necessary and where water and outdoor electrical points could be installed.

Zone or bubble diagram indicating different areas:

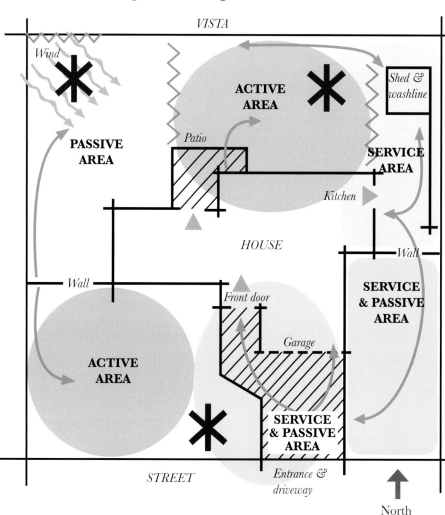

List of invader plants in South Africa *

CATEGORY 1: Invader plants must be removed and destroyed immediately.	CATEGORY 2: Invader plants may be grown under controlled and monitored conditions only.	CATEGORY 3: Invader plants may no longer be planted but kept if existing.

Kind of plant		
Botanical name	**Common Name**	**Category**
Acacia baileyana	Bailey's wattle	3
Acacia cyclops	Rooikrans	2
Acacia dealbata	Silver wattle	Category 1 plant in Western Cape; Category 2 plant in the rest of South Africa
Acacia decurrens	Green wattle	2
Acacia elata	Pepper tree wattle	3
Acacia implexa	Screw-pod wattle	1
Acacia longifolia	Long-leaved wattle	1
Acacia mearnsii	Black wattle	2
Acacia melanoxylon	Australian blackwood	2
Acacia paradoxa	Kangaroo wattle	1
Acacia podalyriifolia	Pearl acacia	3
Acacia pycnantha	Golden wattle	1
Acacia saligna	Port Jackson willow	2
Achyranthes aspera	Burweed	1
Agave sisalana	Sisal hemp, Sisal	2
Ageratina adenophora	Crofton weed	1
Ageratina riparia	Mistflower	1
Ageratum conyzoides	Invading ageratum	1
Ageratum houstonianum	Mexican ageratum	1
Ailanthus altissima	Tree-of-heaven	3
Albizia lebbeck	Lebbeck tree	1
Albizia procera	False lebbeck	1
Alhagi maurorum	Camel thorn bush	1
Anredera cordifolia	Madeira vine, Brida wreath	1
Araujia sericifera	Moth catcher	1
Ardisia crenata	Coralberry tree, Coral bush	Category 1 plant **only** in Northern Province, Kwa Zulu-Natal & Mpumalanga
Argemone mexicana	Yellow-flowered Mexican poppy	1
Argemone ochroleuca	White-flowered Mexican poppy	1
Arundo donax	Giant reed, Spanish reed	1
Atriplex lindley	Sponge-fruit satltbush	3

Atriplex nummularia	Old man saltbush	2
Azolla filiculoides	Red water fern	1
Bauhinia purpurea	Butterfly orchid tree	3
Bauhinia variegata	Orchid tree	3
Bryophyllum delagoense	Chandelier plant	1
Caesalpinia decapetala	Mauritius thorn	1
Campuloclinium macrocephalum	Pom pom weed	1
Canna indica	Indian shot	1
Cardiospermum grandiflorum	Balloon vine	1
Casuarina cunninghamiana	Beefwood	2
Casuarina equisetifolia	Horsetail tree	2
Cereus jamacaru	Queen of the Night	1
Cestrum aurantiacum	Yellow or Orange cestrum	1
Cestrum elegans	Crimson cestrum	1
Cestrum laevgatum Schtdl	Inkberry	1
Cestrum parqui	Chilean cestrum	1
Chromolaena odorata	Triffid weed, Chromolaena	1
Cinnamomum camphora	Camphor tree	Category 1 plant **only** in the Northern Province, KwaZulu-Natal & Mpumalanga
Cirsium vulgare	Spear thistle, Scotch thistle	1
Convolvulus arvensis	Field bindweed, Wild morning glory	1
Cortaderia jubata	Pampas grass	1
Cortaderia selloana	Pampas grass	1
Cotoneaster franchetii	Coloneaster	3
Cotoneaster pannosus	Silver-leaf cotoneaster	3
Cuscuta campestris	Common dodder	1
Cuscuta suaveolens	Lucerne dodder	1
Cytisus monspessulanus	Montpellier broom	1
Cytisus scoparius	Scotch broom	1
Datura ferox	Large thorn apple	1
Datura innoxia	Downy thorn apple	1
Datura stramonium	Common thorn apple	1
Echinopsis spachiana	Torch cactus	1
Echium plantagineum	Patterson's curse	1
Echium vulgare	Blue echium	1

* lists for 2002, which are the ONLY lists that are officially in legislation at time of print

Egeria densa	Dense water weed	1
Eichhornia crassipes	Water hyacinth	1
Elodea canadensis	Canadian water weed	1
Eriobotrya japonica	Loquat	3
Eucalyptus camaldulensis	Red river gum	2
Eucalyptus cladocalyx	Sugar gum	2
Eucalyptus diversicolor	Karri	2
Eucalyptus grandis	Saligna gum, Rose gum	2
Eucalyptus lehmannii	Spider gum	Category 1 plant in the Western Cape; Category 2 plant in the rest of South Africa
Eucalyptus paniculata	Grey ironbark	2
Eucalyptus sideroxylon	Black ironbark, Red ironbark	2
Eugenia uniflora	Pitanga, Surinam cherry	Category 1 plant in the Northern Province, KwaZulu-Natal and Mpumalanga; Category 3 plant in the rest of South Africa
Gleditsia triacanthos	Honey locust, Sweet locust	2
Grevillea robusta	Australian silky oak	3
Hakea drupacea	Sweet hakea	1
Hakea gibbosa	Rock hakea	1
Hakea sericea	Silky hakea	1
Harrisia martinii	Moon cactus, Harrisia cactus	1
Hedychium coccineum	Red ginger lily	1
Hedychium coronarium	White ginger lily	1
Hedychium flavescens	Yellow ginger lily	1
Hedychium gardnerianum	Kahili ginger lily	1
Hypericum perforatum	St.Johns' wort, Tipton weed	2
Ipomoea alba	Moonflower	Category 1 plant in the Northern Province, KwaZulu-Natal & Mpumalanga; Category 3 plant in the rest of South Africa
Ipomoea indica	Morning glory	Category 1 plant in the Northern Province, KwaZulu-Natal & Mpumalanga; Category 3 plant in the rest of South Africa
Ipomoea purpurea	Morning glory	3
Jacaranda mimosifolia	Jacaranda	3
All seed producing species or seed producing hybrids of Lantana that are non-indigenous to Africa	Lantana/Lantana, Tickberry, Cherry Pie	1

Lepidium	Pepper-cres, Hoary cardaria, White top	1
Leptospermum laevigatum	Australian myrtle	1
Leucaena leucocephala	Leucaena	Category 1 plant in the Western Cape; Category 2 plant in South Africa, excluding Western Cape
Ligustrum japonicum	Japanese wax-leaved privet	3
Ligustrum lucidum	Chinese wax-leaved privet	3
Ligustrum ovalifolium	Californian privet	3
Ligustrum sinense	Chinese privet	3
Ligustrum vulgare	Common privet	3
Lilium formosanum	St Joseph's lily, Trumpet lily, Formosa lily	3
Litsea glutinosa	Indian laurel	1
Lyrthrum salicaria	Purple loosestrife	1
Macfadyena unguis-cati	Cat's claw creeper	1
Melia azedarach	"Syringa", Persian lilac	3
Metrosideros excelsa	New Zealand christmas tree	3
Mimosa pigra	Giant sensitive plant	3
Montanoa hibiscifolia	Tree daisy	1
Morus alba	White mulberry, Common mulberry	3
Myoporum tenuifolium	Manatoka	3
Myriophylum aquaticum	Parrot's feather	1
Myriophyllum spicatum	Spiked water - milfoil	1
Nassella tenuissima	White tussock	1
Nassella trichotoma	Nassella tussock	1
Nephrolepis exaltata	Sword fern	3
Nerium oleander	Oleander	1
Nicotiana glauca	Wild tobacco	1
Opuntia aurantiaca	Jointed cactus	1
Opuntia exaltata	Long spine cactus	1
Opuntia	Mission prickly pear, Sweet prickly pear	1
Opuntia humifusa	Large flowered prickly pear, Creeping prickly pear	1
Opuntia imbricata	Imbricate cactus, Imbricate prickly pear	1
Opuntia lindheimeri	Small round-leaved prickly pear	1
Opuntia monacantha	Cochineal prickly pear, Drooping prickly pear	1
Opuntia rosea	Rosea cactus	1
Opuntia spinulifera	Saucepan cactus, Large roundleaved prickly pear	1

Opuntia stricta	Pest pear of Australia	1
Orobanche minor	Lesser broomrape, *Clover broomrape*	1
Paraserianthes lophantha	Austalian Albizia, Stink bean	1
Parthenium hysterophorus	Parthenium	1
Passiflora caerulea	Blue passion flower	1
Passiflora molissima	Banana poka, Bandadilla	1
Passiflora suberosa	Devil's pumpkin, Indigo berry	1
Passiflora subpeltata	Grandina	1
Pennisetum setaceum	Fountain grass	1
Pennisetum villosum	Feathertop	1
Pereskia aculeata	Pereskia/Barbados gooseberry	1
Phytolacca dioica	Belhambra	3
Pinus canariensis	Canary den	2
Pinus elliotti	Slash pine	2
Pinus halepensis	Aleppo pine	2
Pinus patula	Patula pine	2
Pinus pinaster	Cluster pine	2
Pinus radiata	Radiata pine, Monterey pine	2
Pinus roxburghii	Chir pine, *longifolia pine*	2
Pinus taeda	Loblolly pine	2
Pistia stratiotes	Water lettuce	1
Pittosporum undulatum	Australian cheesewood, Sweet pittospormum	1
Plectranthus comosus	Abyssinian' coleus, Wooly plectranthus	3
Pontederia cordata	Pickerel weed	3
Populus alba	White popular	2
Populus x canescens	Grey popular, Matchwood popular	2
Prosopis glandulosa	Honey mesquite	2
Proposis velutina	Velvet mesquite	2
Psidium cattleianum	Strawberry guava	3
Psidium guajava	Guava	2
Psidium guineense	Brazilian guava	3
Psidium x durbanensis	Durban guava	1
Pueraria lobata	Kudu vine	1
Pyrancantha angustifolia	Yellow firethorn	3
Pyrancantha crenulata	Himalayan firethorn	3
Rhus succedanea	Wax tree	1
Ricinus communis	Castor - oil plant	2
Rivina humilis	Rivina, Bloodberry	1
Robinia pseudoacacia	Black locust	2
Rorippa nasturtium - aquaticum	Watercress	2
Rosa rubiginosa	Eglantine, Sweetbriar	1
Rubus cuneifolius	American bramble	1
Rubus fruticosus	European blackberry	2
Salix babylonica	Weeping willow	2
Salix fragilis	Crack or brittle willow	2
Salvinia molesta	Kariba weed	1
Schinus terebinthifolius	Brazilian pepper tree	Category 1 in KwaZulu-Natal Category 3 in the rest of South Africa
Senna bicapsularis	Rambling cassia	3
Senna didymobotrya	Peanut butter cassia	3
Senna pendula		3
Sesbania punicea	Red sesbania	1
Solanum elaeagnifolium	Silver-leaf bitter apple	1
Solanum mauritianum	Bugweed	1
Solanum seaforthianum	Potato creeper	1
Solanum sisymbriifolium	Wild tomato, Dense-thorned bitter apple	2
Sorghum halepense	Johnson grass, Aleppo grass	2
Spartium junceum	Spanish broom	1
Syzygium cumini	Jambolan	3
Syzygium jambos	Rose apple	3
Tamarix chinensis	Chinese tamarisk	Category 1 plant in the Northern, Western and Eastern Cape; Category 3 plant in the rest of South Africa
Tamarix ramosissima	Pink tamarisk	"Category 1 plant in the Northern, Western and Eastern Cape; Category 3 plant in the rest of South Africa
Tecoma stans	Yellow bells	1
Thelechitonia trilobata	Singapore daisy	Category 1 in KwaZulu-Natal; Category 3 plant in the rest of South Africa
Thevetia	Yellow oleander	1
Tipuana tipu	Tipu tree	3
Tithonia diversifolia	Mexican sunflower	1
Tithonia rotundifolia	Red sunflower	1
Toona ciliata	Toon tree	3
Triplaris americana	Indian almond	1
Ulex europaeus	European gorse	1
Xanthium spinosum	Spiny cocklebur	1
Xanthium strumarium	Large cocklebur	1

INDEX